BEYOND THI

THE BELIEVER AND

THE OLD C(

Books by David H.J.Gay referred to in this volume:

*Battle for the Church 1517-1644.*

*Believers Under The Law Of Christ.*

*Christ Is All: No Sanctification by the Law.*

*Christ's Obedience Imputed.*

*Deceit in Death: Christendom in the Raw: 'Christian' Last Rites for Unbelievers.*

*Eternal Justification: Gospel Preaching to Sinners Marred by Hyper-Calvinism.*

*Fivefold Sanctification.*

*Infant Baptism Tested.*

*Letting Loose a Gadfly: Edward Miall Speaks Today.*

*Liberty Not Licence.*

*Positional Sanctification: Two Consequences.*

*Psalm 119 and The New Covenant.*

*Redemption History Through Covenants.*

*The Pastor: Does He Exist?*

*The Priesthood of All Believers: Slogan or Substance?*

*Three Verses Misunderstood: Galatians 3:23-25 Expounded.*

# Beyond the Negative

*The Believer and the Promises of the Old Covenant*

David H.J.Gay

BRACHUS

BRACHUS 2018
davidhjgay@googlemail.com

Scripture quotations come from a variety of versions

All my books, kindles, sermons, audio books, articles and
videos
can be found at davidhjgay.com

# Contents

# *Foreword*

This little book has a long reach and is full of biblical insights of great practical use for Christians today. In fewer than 100 pages, a pleasant evening's read, David Gay explores the connexion between the believer and the promises made to the Israelites in the Old Testament. Perhaps, like me, you have heard or read those who urge us to claim these promises for ourselves. Like Pilate we should ask: 'Am I a Jew?' (John 18:35).

But the risen Lord Jesus Christ pointed his followers back to the law, the prophets and the psalms (Luke 24:44). And the New Testament quotes, builds on and assumes the existence of the Old. How then are we to use the Old Testament responsibly in the age of Christ's church?

The use of the Old Testament is not a dry or academic question. Get this wrong and you will find yourself tied in knots while trying to explain why God does not promise land, health and wealth to Christians. How do you square the prayer of Jabez (1 Chron. 4:10) with Christ's repeated warnings that to follow him [that is, Christ himself] is to invite persecution? Or how do you reconcile that prayer with your own condition at this very moment? Has your territory been enlarged? Have you been kept free from harm and pain? These are personal not theoretical matters. And those who misuse Scripture to promise prosperity or healing dishonour Christ and harm those they hoodwink.

'Consider it pure joy, my brothers and sisters, whenever you face trials of many kinds' is how James begins his letter. He, for one, hadn't understood the so-called prosperity gospel, 'which is really no gospel at all' (Gal. 1:7).

Here is another man who did not buy into it; Richard Baxter, commenting on John 5:5, wrote this: 'How great a mercy it was to live thirty-eight years under God's wholesome discipline! O my God, I thank thee for the like discipline of fifty-eight years; how safe a life is this in comparison with full prosperity and pleasure!'

So I encourage you to read these pages. Read them with your Bible open beside you. Check what has been written against the revealed word of God. And enjoy the blessings of living under the new covenant instituted by the Lord Jesus Christ. His fulfilment of the old covenant reveals what we are to make of the promises and the curses in the Old Testament.

Steve Guest

# Introduction

In this booklet, while what I say has relevance to all believers (and, if any read it, unbelievers), my sights are set mainly on new-covenant theologians. When new-covenant theologians (I include myself) face old-covenant promises, there is a risk of our being content with the negative; that is to say, we can so easily declaim on what these promises do not mean for the believer, and leave it at that. If so, we make a great mistake. For a start, we must surely be acting contrary to Paul's clear assertion on a foundational aspect of the faith:

> All Scripture is breathed out by God and profitable for teaching, for reproof, for correction, and for training in righteousness, that the man of God may be complete, equipped for every good work (2 Tim. 3:16-17).

Yes, all Scripture – every scripture – is profitable for, valuable for, important for, has something to say to, every believer, and to say it today. And this clearly means that we cannot be content to state what certain scriptural promises do not mean for the believer. Our negative may well be right. Nevertheless, questions remain. What should we make of these promises? Being part of the word of God, they must be profitable for believers today. In what way? What do they say to *us* as contemporary believers? What positive use can and should *we* make of such promises?[1]

This is what I want to try to deal with in this booklet.

Before I do, I record my thanks to Steve Guest for his Foreword. I am grateful for his endorsement of this little work. May both our hopes be realised in the profit of many readers.

---

[1] As we go on, I will say a little more about the way the new covenant uses the law and the prophets.

# The Issue

The word of God is explicit:

> When I shut up the heavens so that there is no rain, or command the locust to devour the land, or send pestilence among my people, if my people who are called by my name humble themselves, and pray and seek my face and turn from their wicked ways, then I will hear from heaven and will forgive their sin and heal their land (2 Chron. 7:13-14).

Again:

> 'Bring the full tithe into the storehouse, that there may be food in my house. And thereby put me to the test', says the LORD of hosts, 'if I will not open the windows of heaven for you and pour down for you a blessing until there is no more need. I will rebuke the devourer for you, so that it will not destroy the fruits of your soil, and your vine in the field shall not fail to bear', says the LORD of hosts. 'Then all nations will call you blessed, for you will be a land of delight', says the LORD of hosts (Mal. 3:10-12).

Here we have two of the countless promises given to the people of God in Scripture. Here we have the dogmatic assurance that if we, as believers, meet the conditions and call upon God in the right way, he will send us such blessing – revival, indeed – that we shall be like those that dream (Ps. 126:1).

So many believe. So they argue. So they assure believers who are willing to listen to them. Are they right?

Most definitely, they are not!

Oh? Don't all the promises of Scripture belong to us?

Well, no, they don't. What? No, it is simply not true to say that all the promises written in the Bible are recorded for us, as believers, living in the days of the new covenant, to 'claim'. Not at all. Staggering as that may sound to some, it is the truth. Incidentally, I myself do not like the idea of 'claim'. I prefer 'plead'. But I let the 'claim' stand.

Let me pause for a moment to justify my assertion by broadening the point. Not all the promises are recorded in Scripture for believers to claim. The same applies to the commandments. Specific commands to specific individuals for a specific purpose are not recorded in Scripture for the believer to claim. Take Genesis 12:1-3. Abram was commanded to leave home, not knowing where he was going, and in this way God would make him into a great nation. Both the command and its associated promise were given specifically to Abram, not set out for believers to claim today. As for the law of Moses, believers are not bound by the laws of Leviticus 19:19, for instance. This does not mean such passages have no relevance for the believer. They do. They come under 2 Timothy 3:16-17. But believers do not have to obey these commandments. They are not given to them. Indeed, believers are delivered from the Mosaic covenant, the law (Rom. 6:14 – 7:6; 2 Cor. 3:6-11; Galatians; Hebrews, for instance). Nevertheless, the law is still profitable for them as a paradigm and illustration of the gospel, and the life of the believer. This is how the apostles used them.[2]

And this is true of the promises we are talking about. Consider these promises:

> Blessed is the man who walks not in the counsel of the wicked, nor stands in the way of sinners, nor sits in the seat of scoffers; but his delight is in the law of the LORD, and on his law he meditates day and night. He is like a tree planted by streams of water that yields its fruit in its season, and its leaf does not wither. In all that he does, he prospers (Ps. 1:1-3).

> The rules [just decrees] of the LORD are true, and righteous altogether. More to be desired are they than gold, even

---

[2] Rom. 13:8-10; Gal. 5:14-15; Eph. 6:1-4. See my *Christ Is All*; 'No Mixture! Separation!'; 'NCT Made Simple: Separation Essential: No Mixture! Deut. 22:9-11'. I will return to this.

much fine gold; sweeter also than honey and drippings of the honeycomb. Moreover, by them is your servant warned; in keeping them there is great reward (Ps. 19:9-11).

The eye of the LORD is on those who fear him, on those who hope in his steadfast love, that he may deliver their soul from death and keep them alive in famine (Ps. 33:18-19).

When the righteous cry for help, the LORD hears and delivers them out of all their troubles... Many are the afflictions of the righteous, but the LORD delivers him out of them all. He keeps all his bones; not one of them is broken (Ps. 34:17,19-20).

Blessed is the one who considers the poor! In the day of trouble the LORD delivers him; the LORD protects him and keeps him alive; he is called blessed in the land; you do not give him up to the will of his enemies. The LORD sustains him on his sick bed; in his illness you restore him to full health (Ps. 41:1-3).

The LORD... heals all your diseases (Ps. 103:2-3).

If these promises, and countless others like them,[3] apply, as they stand, to us as believers today, then we have to understand that, if they meet the conditions laid down, true believers will always prosper in everything they set their hand to; that godly men and women will never suffer in any time of want or famine; that believers will always be delivered out of every trouble; that never, under any circumstances, will a believer break a bone; that no believer will ever be ill or, at the very least, will always be healed whatever disease stalks the land. And so on. Those who hold to what is known as the prosperity gospel, the health-and-wealth gospel, claim it is so.

Of course, it might well be argued that all those believers who suffer, and do not get the promised answer to their prayer, do so simply because they fail to meet the conditions. That is to say, they suffer because they have committed

---

[3] Take, as just one example, the book of Haggai.

some sin and are tolerating it, that they just do not come up to scratch, they do not meet the stipulated conditions.

Well, it might be so, I agree. But is it always the case? And what if it is not the case? After all, don't some, if not most, believers – even the most faithful of believers – fall ill from time to time? Don't some godly men and women die young? Don't true believers always suffer persecution, don't they *inevitably* suffer persecution – this being an integral concomitant of being in Christ (Matt. 10:16-22; 24:9; John 15:18-20; Rom. 8:17; 2 Cor. 1:3-11; 4:7-11; 2 Tim. 1:8,12; 2:3,9-14; 3:1; 4:5, for instance)? Isn't chastisement, as part of progressive sanctification, an essential aspect of the believer's life, a mark of his being a true child of God, of his being disciplined for his profit by a loving Father (Heb. 12:1-14)?[4] Don't all believers age? Doesn't their ageing show, both inwardly and outwardly? Don't many godly people suffer bereavement? Don't all believers have to face setback and disappointment? Haven't many prophets and countless martyrs been put through harrowing torture which has led to an indescribably painful death? Aren't saints suffering for Christ even now? And so on.

I ask these rhetorical questions to stress that these things are facts, indisputable facts, hard, stubborn facts. And no amount of fudging will get round them, or put a stop to them. The Cnut (Canute) of popular but mythical understanding might think he could stop the tide, but the truth is the exact

---

[4] The incense of the old covenant had to be beaten and pounded in order to extract its essence, and then subjected to fire so that the sweetness of its perfume might ascend to God. Is this, in part, an illustration of the discipline to which God subjects each of his children (Heb. 12:5-11)? I think so. Some plants only give up their perfume after they have been crushed. A camomile lawn yields its sweet fragrance after being bruised as it is walked on and trodden down. John Gill commenting on Ex. 30:25, spoke of the anointing oil as 'an ointment compounded after the art of the apothecary, or confectioner; the spices bruised, and pounded, and mixed together, and boiled or distilled, and so an oil or ointment [is] extracted from them'.

opposite; he was, in fact, demonstrating that he had no power to stop it! So it is with suffering affliction, even by believers. Eliphaz got it right: 'Man [not excluding the best of believers] is born to trouble as the sparks fly upward' (Job 5:7). And this, of course, was as a result of man's fall in Adam. God cursed the woman:

> I will surely multiply your pain in childbearing; in pain you shall bring forth children. Your desire shall be towards [see Gen. 4:7] your husband, but he shall rule over you (Gen. 3:16).

> Because you have listened to the voice of your wife and have eaten of the tree of which I commanded you: 'You shall not eat of it', cursed is the ground because of you; in pain you shall eat of it all the days of your life; thorns and thistles it shall bring forth for you; and you shall eat the plants of the field. By the sweat of your face you shall eat bread, till you return to the ground, for out of it you were taken; for you are dust, and to dust you shall return (Gen. 3:17-19).

Believers are not exempt:

> I consider that the sufferings of this present time are not worth comparing with the glory that is to be revealed to us. For the creation waits with eager longing for the revealing of the sons of God. For the creation was subjected to futility, not willingly, but because of him who subjected it, in hope that the creation itself will be set free from its bondage to corruption and obtain the freedom of the glory of the children of God. For we know that the whole creation has been groaning together in the pains of childbirth until now. And not only the creation, but we ourselves, who have the firstfruits of the Spirit, groan inwardly as we wait eagerly for adoption as sons, the redemption of our bodies. For in this hope we were saved. Now hope that is seen is not hope. For who hopes for what he sees? But if we hope for what we do not see, we wait for it with patience (Rom. 8:18-25).

Yes, man is born to affliction. Changing the illustration, like the Mississippi, troubles just keep rolling along. And, I might add, rolling our way. No believer is exempt; no, not the most godly of believers.

So, if the prosperity-gospel teacher tells a suffering believer that he is suffering because of his sin when he is not, he is compounding the believer's trouble, adding to it, rubbing salt into an open wound. The believer is not only suffering, but now he has to stumble on with the added burden of blaming himself for his trouble, knowing that others are pointing the finger at him. This must be a sure-fire recipe for a whirlpool of depression and grief, taking us into a very different atmosphere to that of the New Testament and the new covenant; that is, I fail to discover such believers in the New Testament, believers who, though claiming the promises, are suffering because they are failing to meet the conditions.[5]

Could there be a better illustration of this than Job's comforters? Although they pre-dated the old covenant, they certainly plugged the prosperity gospel. Time and again they rubbed Job's nose in it (Job 4:7-9; 5:19-27; 8:1-22; 11:13-20; 18:5-35; 20:4-29; 22:4-30; 36:11-15). And we all know how wide of the mark they were in Job's case! Of course, they were not above contradicting themselves, allowing that there is no simple answer to the exigencies of life (see Job 5:7; 14:1-6; 21:23-24).

I hinted there could be no better illustration. But what about the Lord Jesus Christ himself? Did he not suffer at the hands of prosperity gospellers? I can hear its undertones in such taunts as are recorded in Matthew 27:39-44,49. One of the men crucified with him did get the point, however (Luke 23:39-43), as did the centurion (Luke 23:47).

And surely the attempt to justify the prosperity gospel must hit the buffers by the account of Paul's thorn in the flesh. The apostle had been granted precious revelation by Christ. But it came with a price tag:

---

[5] I am speaking as precisely as I can. I will return to curses in the new covenant.

To keep me from becoming conceited because of the surpassing greatness of the revelations, a thorn was given me in the flesh, a messenger of Satan to harass me, to keep me from becoming conceited. Three times I pleaded with the Lord about this, that it should leave me. But he said to me: 'My grace is sufficient for you, for my power is made perfect in weakness'. Therefore I will boast all the more gladly of my weaknesses, so that the power of Christ may rest upon me. For the sake of Christ, then, I am content with weaknesses, insults, hardships, persecutions, and calamities. For when I am weak, then I am strong (2 Cor. 12:7-10).

Whatever this 'thorn in the flesh' was, it was, to say the very least, a physical nuisance for the apostle, one which he earnestly wished to be rid of. He did not pretend. He did not hide the fact. As he told us, he prayed earnestly for its removal. Clearly, he had no notion of the prosperity gospel. If he had been of that persuasion, if he knew that he could 'claim the promise' and be relieved of his trying disability, he would never have needed to write as he did. Indeed, Christ would never have needed to reassure the apostle, giving him his glorious promise of overcoming grace to help him face, live with and overcome his affliction, an affliction which was not going to go away. It would not go away because Christ would not take it away. He had a greater, higher purpose in holding the apostle under the affliction. It wasn't that Paul was ungodly, cherishing unconfessed sin, or anything of the kind. He wasn't 'failing to meet the conditions'. No, Christ had a good purpose in the abiding thorn in the apostle's flesh. Think of the loss, both to Paul himself, and to subsequent generations of believers, if none of this had happened! Think what both he and they – including us believers today – would have missed of Christ's grace![6]

Paul's experience tells us that the new-covenant sense of what is truly valuable and precious – the felt sense of the

---

[6] I will return to this episode.

grace of Christ, for instance – knocks the old-covenant values – of health, for instance – into a cocked hat!

Connected with all that, think of this:

> Blessed be the God and Father of our Lord Jesus Christ, the Father of mercies and God of all comfort, who comforts us in all our affliction, so that we may be able to comfort those who are in any affliction, with the comfort with which we ourselves are comforted by God. For as we share abundantly in Christ's sufferings, so through Christ we share abundantly in comfort too. If we are afflicted, it is for your comfort and salvation; and if we are comforted, it is for your comfort, which you experience when you patiently endure the same sufferings that we suffer. Our hope for you is unshaken, for we know that as you share in our sufferings, you will also share in our comfort (2 Cor. 1:3-7).

The prosperity gospel, at a stroke, destroys this biblical principle.

Again:

> For even when we came into Macedonia, our bodies had no rest, but we were afflicted at every turn – fighting without and fear within. But God, who comforts the downcast, comforted us by the coming of Titus, and not only by his coming but also by the comfort with which he was comforted by you, as he told us of your longing, your mourning, your zeal for me, so that I rejoiced still more. For even if I made you grieve with my letter, I do not regret it – though I did regret it, for I see that that letter grieved you, though only for a while. As it is, I rejoice, not because you were grieved, but because you were grieved into repenting. For you felt a godly grief, so that you suffered no loss through us. For godly grief produces a repentance that leads to salvation without regret, whereas worldly grief produces death. For see what earnestness this godly grief has produced in you, but also what eagerness to clear yourselves, what indignation, what fear, what longing, what zeal, what punishment! At every point you have proved yourselves innocent in the matter. So although I wrote to you, it was not for the sake of the one who did the wrong, nor for the sake of the one who suffered the wrong, but in order that your earnestness for us might be revealed to you in the sight of God. Therefore we are comforted. And

besides our own comfort, we rejoiced still more at the joy of Titus, because his spirit has been refreshed by you all. For whatever boasts I made to him about you, I was not put to shame. But just as everything we said to you was true, so also our boasting before Titus has proved true. And his affection for you is even greater, as he remembers the obedience of you all, how you received him with fear and trembling. I rejoice, because I have complete confidence in you (2 Cor. 7:5-16).

Yet again, sorrow, and mutual comfort in sorrow, sweetly joined. No prosperity gospel here!

Reflect on Paul's reaction to his imprisonment for Christ. Although he was cut off from his heart's delight – preaching the gospel – nevertheless, he rejoiced! He rejoiced because through his imprisonment people in the upper echelons of Roman society – particularly the military – were talking about Paul, and this inevitably meant talking about Christ. Not only that. The majority of believers who were watching drew courage from Paul's sufferings and privations, and were moved to preach Christ even more freely than before. True, some did it with the wrong motive, wanting to rub brine into the apostle's raw wounds, but even then he rejoiced. Why? Because, whether from good motives or bad, Christ was preached, and all because of his loss:

I want you to know, brothers, that what has happened to me has really served to advance the gospel, so that it has become known throughout the whole imperial guard and to all the rest that my imprisonment is for Christ. And most of the brothers, having become confident in the Lord by my imprisonment, are much more bold to speak the word without fear. Some indeed preach Christ from envy and rivalry, but others from good will. The latter do it out of love, knowing that I am put here for the defence of the gospel. The former proclaim Christ out of selfish ambition, not sincerely but thinking to afflict me in my imprisonment. What then? Only that in every way, whether in pretence or in truth, Christ is proclaimed, and in that I rejoice (Phil. 1:12-18).

He went on:

Yes, and I will rejoice, for I know that through your prayers
and the help of the Spirit of Jesus Christ this will turn out
for my deliverance... (Phil. 1:18-19)

Ah! See? Deliverance because of prayer! The prosperity
gospel after all!

Not a bit of it! 'Deliverance' (*sōtēria*) means
'deliverance, preservation, safety, salvation'. What Paul is
*not* doing here is bragging about certain rescue and the
reinstatement of his liberty with attendant opportunities for
preaching. Not at all. He might even be thinking of his
eternal reward. See how he goes on:

Yes, and I will rejoice, for I know that through your prayers
and the help of the Spirit of Jesus Christ this will turn out
for my deliverance, as it is my eager expectation and hope
that I will not be at all ashamed, but that with full courage
now as always Christ will be honoured in my body, whether
by life or by death. For to me to live is Christ, and to die is
gain. If I am to live in the flesh, that means fruitful labour
for me. Yet which I shall choose I cannot tell. I am hard
pressed between the two. My desire is to depart and be with
Christ, for that is far better. But to remain in the flesh is
more necessary on your account. Convinced of this, I know
that I will remain and continue with you all, for your
progress and joy in the faith, so that in me you may have
ample cause to glory in Christ Jesus, because of my coming
to you again (Phil. 1:18-26).

And look how he turned his sufferings into a preaching
opportunity, and note what use he made of it in his
application to fellow-believers both then and now:

Only let your manner of life be worthy of the gospel of
Christ, so that whether I come and see you or am absent, I
may hear of you that you are standing firm in one spirit,
with one mind striving side by side for the faith of the
gospel, and not frightened in anything by your opponents.
This is a clear sign to them of their destruction, but of your
salvation, and that from God. For it has been granted to you
that for the sake of Christ you should not only believe in
him but also suffer for his sake, engaged in the same

conflict that you saw I had and now hear that I still have (Phil. 1:27-30).

Yet again, the prosperity gospel effectively expunges from Scripture all these spiritual gains which accrue through suffering.

Consider Paul's advice to Timothy concerning his chronic digestive problem (1 Tim. 5:23). Think of his inability to relieve Trophimus in his illness, despite his concern for his sick brother (2 Tim. 4:20). And then we have this:

> You know it was because of a bodily ailment that I preached the gospel to you at first, and though my condition was a trial to you, you did not scorn or despise me, but received me as an angel of God, as Christ Jesus. What then has become of your blessedness? For I testify to you that, if possible, you would have gouged out your eyes and given them to me (Gal. 4:13-15).

And this:

> I was with you in weakness and in fear and much trembling (1 Cor. 2:3).

And this:

> So we do not lose heart. Though our outer self is wasting away, our inner self is being renewed day by day. For this light momentary affliction is preparing for us an eternal weight of glory beyond all comparison, as we look not to the things that are seen but to the things that are unseen. For the things that are seen are transient, but the things that are unseen are eternal. For we know that if the tent that is our earthly home is destroyed, we have a building from God, a house not made with hands, eternal in the heavens. For in this tent we groan, longing to put on our heavenly dwelling, if indeed by putting it on we may not be found naked. For while we are still in this tent, we groan, being burdened – not that we would be unclothed, but that we would be further clothed, so that what is mortal may be swallowed up by life. He who has prepared us for this very thing is God, who has given us the Spirit as a guarantee.

So we are always of good courage. We know that while we are at home in the body we are away from the Lord, for we walk by faith, not by sight. Yes, we are of good courage, and we would rather be away from the body and at home with the Lord. So whether we are at home or away, we make it our aim to please him. For we must all appear before the judgment seat of Christ, so that each one may receive what is due for what he has done in the body, whether good or evil (2 Cor. 4:16 – 5:10).

As servants of God we commend ourselves in every way: by great endurance, in afflictions, hardships, calamities, beatings, imprisonments, riots, labours, sleepless nights, hunger; by purity, knowledge, patience, kindness, the Holy Spirit, genuine love; by truthful speech, and the power of God; with the weapons of righteousness for the right hand and for the left; through honour and dishonour, through slander and praise. We are treated as impostors, and yet are true; as unknown, and yet well known; as dying, and behold, we live; as punished, and yet not killed; as sorrowful, yet always rejoicing; as poor, yet making many rich; as having nothing, yet possessing everything (2 Cor. 6:4-10).

Count it all joy, my brothers, when you meet trials of various kinds, for you know that the testing of your faith produces steadfastness. And let steadfastness have its full effect, that you may be perfect and complete, lacking in nothing... Blessed is the man who remains steadfast under trial, for when he has stood the test he will receive the crown of life, which God has promised to those who love him (Jas. 1:2-4,12).

In this [that is, salvation] you rejoice, though now for a little while, if necessary, you have been grieved by various trials, so that the tested genuineness of your faith – more precious than gold that perishes though it is tested by fire – may be found to result in praise and glory and honour at the revelation of Jesus Christ (1 Pet. 1:6-7).

And so on.

Is it not clear? The prosperity gospel is nothing but a cruel delusion; cruel, I say. Cruel because, as I have remarked, it adds to the sufferer's pain, adds to it by putting into his mind, heart and conscience the grim thought that he is going through this needless experience because of unconfessed sin, or because he fails to 'meet the conditions', when all the time it might well be the way in which Christ is supplying grace to him. It might well be a token of mercy, a sign of blessing!

The cost – emotional, psychological, physical, spiritual – for those who buy into the prosperity gospel is immense. The damage can be permanent. And I mean permanent, both in this life and eternity. Numberless scarred victims, I am convinced, are stumbling along with it even at this moment. What do such believers do when all things fall apart – as they do! After all, who doesn't sing: 'When all around my soul gives way'? That's the real question. What happens then? Believers don't always have good health. Some godly men and women die young. Prosperity gospellers attend funerals of believers, some of whom have experienced what most would consider to be untimely deaths. Indeed, some prosperity gospellers undergo such a death themselves. Believers fall ill. They meet setbacks. Oh yes they do, whatever they say to the contrary.

Prosperity-gospel teaching is a scam. It is a con. It is bolstered by subterfuge, and can only be supported by the telling of blatant lies. The evidence is there for all to see. I have come across the most fantastic attempts at damage limitation, even the telling of barefaced lies, in an effort to skirt round the experienced failure. This brings nothing but disrepute – disrepute, I repeat – on the cause and person of Christ. The prosperity gospellers may kid themselves, but the man in the street is not fooled. He can detect whistling in the dark when he hears it. Let me give two examples of what I mean by subterfuge and lies.

I know of a leading proponent of prosperity-gospel teaching whose wife, alas, was dying of cancer. She claimed the victory, climbed out of bed, staggered a few steps before she fell, dead. The husband, however, boasted that she had the victory, that she was cured, cured according to the promise they were claiming, cured just before she died.

Really, if things were not so serious they would be laughable. The world, on hearing such nonsense, would rightly laugh it out of court. Worse, they would lump Christ and the Scriptures with the preposterous claim and laugh it all out of court.

Again, a godly man I knew had cancer. The church held special, protracted prayer meetings – nights and half-nights at a time. But he died. Even so, the leaders were able to reassure all and sundry – I might almost say they crowed about it – that they had the desired and expected answer: 'Our brother had the perfect cure'. My father saw through the lie for what it was worth, which was less than nothing; it was a sham. 'This is not what we were praying for', he dryly observed. It was yet another case of the emperor's clothes (or lack of them). In any case, according to the promise being 'claimed', there was no need for the church to spend all or half-nights in prayer. The promises they were 'claiming' made no mention of anything of the sort.

Let us get down to brass tacks and inject a good dose of biblical sanity into this cruel and shoddy farrago.

It is all based on a puerile mistake of biblical interpretation. The prosperity-gospel teachers are ignorant of a basic point of biblical interpretation. Or else they deliberately turn a blind eye to it. In the following chapter I will explore this.

But before I bring this chapter to a close, may I explain what drives me to produce this small work. I am moved by the way, through a grievous, basic misunderstanding of how to read Scripture, many believers are taken into dreadful – literally dreadful – experiences of anguish, self-doubt and torment, grievous experiences which can blight their lives for decades. And all because of a basic – elementary – mistake of biblical interpretation. Moreover, unbelievers who listen to men who preach on the basis of the prosperity gospel can easily run away with the appalling misunderstanding – the error – that salvation is by works.

Indeed, as I will show, adopting the principles of the prosperity gospel makes this inevitable.

And this leads me to make what I consider to be a point of the first magnitude. I am not writing and publishing this booklet to move a few pieces on some theological chessboard. Not at all. As in all my works – preaching and publishing – I am concerned with setting out the truth *for the pastoral benefit of those who hear or read what I produce.* What I mean is, my first concern is with Scripture, yes, but for me a proper view of Scripture, not as an end in itself. No! I want to be clear as to what Scripture is really teaching in order to apply it to the everlasting spiritual welfare of the saints (believers) – and the sinners (unbelievers), if any – who hear me or read my works. Such is my concern here.

I am convinced that such a little work is needed. I know there are many excellent volumes and articles on the subject, but if I can do anything to help any child of God in difficulty over the issue, then I must publish. In addition, I hope that any new-covenant theologian who has been content to stop short with pointing out the negative about the prosperity gospel will be encouraged to say more on the positive side. And there is plenty to be said. There must be. For as we know, all Scripture is profitable, profitable for us today. So let us make sure we do what we can to set out the profit to be gained by contemporary believers when they read the promises of the old covenant.

# The Fundamental Point

'Every promise is yours. Claim it now'. So runs the jargon. And it is wrong! It falls at the first and most important fence. I am speaking of a fundamental point of biblical interpretation. Perhaps it would be more accurate to speak of it as *the* fundamental point of biblical interpretation.

*The fundamental point of biblical interpretation.* How should we, as believers, use biblical promises? Should we just claim them? After all, there they are in the Bible, and don't all the promises belong to us? Now this is only a part of a bigger question. How should we read the Bible? But let me stick with the promises. Don't all the promises belong to us? They do, don't they?

Well, no, they don't. What? No, we cannot say that all the promises written in the Bible are there for us to 'claim'. Not at all.

In reading the Bible, we must never forget one of the most vital aspects of revelation. The context is king! The context is always king! Always! In particular, we must always bear in mind the Bible's time-line, where this passage lies in the Bible, which age does it belong to, which covenant reigns at the time, and so on. Then again, if God gives a specific promise to a specific person or persons at a specific time for a specific purpose, what right have we to wrench that promise from its scriptural moorings, and claim it?

None at all!

Going down that road is to make one of the most crass of all mistakes in reading the Bible. The use of a promise box, which at one time was so popular,[7] and which I thought must have disappeared some time during the 60s, is, I find, still

---

[7] I confess that, for a short while, my wife and I had such a box in the 60s. Pure ignorance!

alive and kicking. And if not the practice, then, I am afraid, the thinking behind it is – very much so.

Promise box? A promise box is a decorated carton containing rolls of paper which can be lifted out with a pair of tweezers one at a time, each roll having a promise written on it. While there was – and is, it seems – a ready market for such a box, nobody (surprise, surprise!) ever seems to have thought of trying to market a 'duty box'. In any case, the principle is utterly wrong. The ever-popular Samuel Bagster's *Daily Light on the Daily Path* makes the same mistake. We cannot simply claim promises, whether one by one or in combination, regardless of the context in which they are located in Scripture. No matter how many glowing claims are made for the blessing received by such a practice, nor any amount of 'prettification' of the box, no weight of flowery, sentimental recommendation of the idea, will justify the immature action.

Here's one such blurb: 'Boxes Of Blessings – 101 Bible Promises For Your Every Need'. And here's the recommendation of another:

> The promise box is one of the tools Christians have developed to aid spiritual growth. The idea is simple: a box filled with cards or slips of paper printed with Bible verses. Each day you draw a different card to read, mark, and inwardly digest. The purpose is serious, but the practice is enjoyable. It's a bit like opening a fortune cookie or a birthday present: you never know exactly what you'll get. As you reach for the card you wonder: 'What message does God have for me today?'

Opening a fortune cookie? One definition of a fortune cookie reads like this: 'A fortune cookie is a small biscuit containing a slip of paper with a prediction or motto written on it, served in Chinese restaurants'.[8] Next door to superstition, I should say! Opening a fortune cookie! I ask you! Is that why – taking one example only – William

---

[8] Fortune cookies are a Japanese *cum* American invention, not Chinese.

Tyndale spent and, at the end, gave his life? To translate the Bible (or as much as he could of it) into English so that believers could produce a box of spiritual fortune cookies? More, is this why the Holy Spirit inspired men to write the God-breathed Scriptures (2 Tim. 3:16; 2 Pet. 1:21)? Are we really meant to use the word of God as a lucky dip or bran tub to 'aid [our] spiritual growth'? The result will be quite the opposite. So wacky a rigmarole can only encourage a loose, carnal attitude to Scripture. The mind boggles! At least, mine does. Ludicrous, is it not? What a dreadful mishandling of Scripture! Its damaging ripples will spread far and wide, and be long-lasting.

As I said at the close of the previous chapter, it is high time we injected a note of sanity into this discussion. And that note of sanity is to do with God's revelation of redemption through covenants.[9] This is what I was referring to when I spoke of the Bible's time-line, and the covenants.

No! Don't switch off.

The Bible makes it as plain as plain can be that God, in forming Abraham's descendants through Isaac and Jacob into the nation of Israel, gave them a covenant, with his law at the centre of it. He gave them this covenant at Sinai after using Moses to deliver his people, in the exodus, from centuries of slavery in Egypt.

It came about in this way: under God, Israel became a nation in Egypt (Gen. 46:3; Deut. 26:5), particularly at the exodus leading to Sinai (Gen. 12:1-2; 17:2-14; 46:3,26-27; Ex. 1:5,7; 2:24-25; 3:6-8,10,15-18; 4:5,22-23; 6:2-8; 7:4,16; 8:1; 9:1; 12:2,17; 13:3-10; 15:11-18,26; 16:22-30; 18:1; 19:3-6; 31:13-17; 32:11-14; 33:13; Deut. 4:20,34; 16:1; 27:9; 28:9; Ps. 114:1-2; Ezek. 20:5-12,20; Acts 7:14,17), God confirming Israel's nationhood at the giving of the covenant just before entering Canaan (Deut. 26:18; 27:9). In delivering his people from Egypt, God distinguished them

---

[9] See my *Redemption*.

31

from all other nations by starting their calendar, giving them the feasts and the sabbath as an integral part of his law. 'What great nation is there that has such statutes and righteous judgments as are in all this law which I set before you this day?' (Deut. 4:8). 'For what great nation is there that has a god so near to it as the LORD our God is to us, whenever we call upon him?' (Deut. 4:7) shows the same in his nearness to Israel and his willingness to hear their prayers. In short:

> For ask now of the days that are past, which were before you, since the day that God created man on the earth, and ask from one end of heaven to the other, whether such a great thing as this has ever happened or was ever heard of. Did any people ever hear the voice of a god speaking out of the midst of the fire, as you have heard, and still live? Or has any god ever attempted to go and take a nation for himself from the midst of another nation, by trials, by signs, by wonders, and by war, by a mighty hand and an outstretched arm, and by great deeds of terror, all of which the LORD your God did for you in Egypt before your eyes? To you it was shown, that you might know that the LORD is God; there is no other besides him. Out of heaven he let you hear his voice, that he might discipline you. And on earth he let you see his great fire, and you heard his words out of the midst of the fire. And because he loved your fathers and chose their offspring after them and brought you out of Egypt with his own presence, by his great power, driving out before you nations greater and mightier than you, to bring you in, to give you their land for an inheritance, as it is this day, know therefore today, and lay it to your heart, that the LORD is God in heaven above and on the earth beneath; there is no other. Therefore you shall keep his statutes and his commandments, which I command you today, that it may go well with you and with your children after you, and that you may prolong your days in the land that the LORD your God is giving you for all time (Deut. 4:32-40).

Take the sabbath. Although God could say: 'All the earth is mine', he chose to declare to the Israelites, and only to the Israelites: 'You shall be a special treasure to me above all people'. But there was a condition: 'Now therefore, *if* you will indeed obey my voice and keep my covenant, *then* you shall be a special treasure to me above all people' (Ex. 19:5). 'Keep my covenant'. In other words: 'Keep my law'. In giving this new nation – this nation of Israel, his nation – his law in order to mark them out as his people, God in particular gave them a special – unique – sign that they were his people. This sign belonged to no other people, since only Israel was his nation. And this sign was his sabbaths: 'Moreover I also gave them my sabbaths, to be a sign between them and me, that they might know that I am the LORD who sanctifies them' (Ezek. 20:12); that is, separates them from all other peoples.[10] God commanded the Jews: 'Hallow my sabbaths, and they will be a sign between me and you, that you may know that I am the LORD your God' (Ezek. 20:20). And the same applied to their following generations (Ex. 31:13). By 'sabbaths', of course, God primarily meant the weekly sabbaths, but he also included all the special sabbaths. In short, God commanded the Hebrew people from that time on to keep his law – including the sabbath – especially the sabbath – *and especially the sabbath as a sign that they were God's nation, distinct from all others*:

> Surely my sabbaths you shall keep, for it is a sign between me and you throughout your generations, that you may know that it is the LORD who sanctifies you. You shall keep the sabbath, therefore, for it is holy to you. Everyone who profanes it shall surely be put to death... Work shall be done for six days, but the seventh is the sabbath of rest, holy to the LORD. Whoever does any work on the sabbath day, he shall surely be put to death. Therefore the children of Israel shall keep the sabbath, to observe the sabbath throughout their generations as a perpetual covenant. It is a sign between me and the children of Israel for ever; for in six days the LORD made the heavens and the earth, and on the seventh day he rested and was refreshed (Ex. 31:13-17).

Israel's position was *unique*, not merely *special*.

---

[10] The root meaning of 'sanctify' is 'separate'. See my *Fivefold*.

Taking up the Deuteronomy thread once again, we can see at once that the things God promised to Israel are clearly contrasted with the creation-gift of beasts, birds, fish, planets and the like 'which the LORD your God has given to all the peoples under the whole heaven as a heritage' (Deut. 4:17-19). The contrast is enforced further: 'But the LORD has taken you and brought you [that is, Israel] out of the iron furnace, out of Egypt, to be his people, an inheritance' (Deut. 4:20). Again, as the Lord made clear to the people:

> If you will diligently listen to the voice of the LORD your God, and do that which is right in his eyes, and give ear to his commandments and keep all his statutes, I will put none of the diseases on you that I put on the Egyptians, for I am the LORD, your healer (Ex. 15:26).

And, as I say, one of the greatest distinctions God made between Israel and all other nations was to give his covenant with its law through Moses to Israel – and to no others. The Mosaic covenant with its law divided, separated, Israel from all other people (Deut. 4:1 – 5:33; 7:8-12; Ps. 147:19-20; Rom. 2:12-14; 9:4; 1 Cor. 9:20-21). What did this mean? God, having formed his nation and given them his law in the Mosaic covenant, would deal with Israel – and Israel only – under the terms of that covenant. The Mosaic covenant, its law and its promises, were for Israel, and for Israel only.

What is more, as the Bible makes clear, that covenant and its law for Israel would be in place until the appointed time (appointed by God, that is) of Christ's appearance under that covenant and its law, when he would fulfil and render it obsolete, by bringing in the new covenant. See Galatians 3:23-25, in the proper translation.[11] Indeed, the Bible teaches that the old covenant – the Mosaic covenant and its law with Israel – was not only temporary, but it was a covenant of shadow and type. It foreshadowed, illustrated, the new covenant which Christ would establish. More especially, it foreshadowed and typified Christ himself. Whether land, temple or tabernacle, priest, offering, sacrifice, sabbath,

---

[11] See my *Three.*

feasts, rites or ceremonies... all belonged to Israel, only to Israel. But all were ineffectual. Even so, that covenant and its shadows played a vital role in the history of redemption revealed by God. It all foreshadowed the reality that he, from eternity, decreed would come in and through the person and work of Christ, the One who would fulfil the Mosaic covenant, render it obsolete and thus bring in the new covenant.

Indeed, all this is actually better expressed the other way round. The old covenant reflected the eternal truth, portraying it in shadow to Israel until Christ fulfilled it and brought in the new covenant. For God warned Moses expressly to make sure that everything in the old covenant was securely based on the true heavenly covenant (Ex. 25:40; Heb. 8:5; 9:23; 10:1; see also Col. 2:17). And when he brought in the new covenant, God went back to the old to teach his people the spiritual and heavenly realities of the new covenant in Christ. This was one of the major purposes of God's giving Israel the old covenant. But all along, his intention had been the coming of Christ and the new covenant.

This meant that the nation of Israel was a temporary – essentially an old-covenant – vehicle to carry the covenant and its law, the prophets, and, ultimately the Christ. In Christ all the shadows fell, having been rendered obsolete since they are fulfilled by and in him. There is no special nation now – no Jew or Greek. The reality of the shadows belongs to the new Israel, 'the Israel of God' (Gal. 6:16; see also Rom. 2:28-29; 9:6; Gal. 3:7,29; Phil. 3:3; 1 Pet. 2:9-10). No post-Pentecost scripture speaks of Israel as a nation in the land. Or returning to the land. Not one! Of course, 'Israel' passages are quoted (as above), but they are always applied to believers, as being the new-covenant fulfilment of the old-covenant shadow, unless, it goes without saying, the apostle wants to speak of Israel in a historical sense – see, for example, 1 Corinthians 10:1-13,18; 2 Corinthians 3:7,13-15; 11:22; Philippians 3:4-5 .

The newness of the new covenant is an essential aspect of all its constituents. It is a new covenant with a new people (Heb. 8:8-13; 10:14-18), all of whom have a new heart by the Spirit (Ezek. 11:19; 36:26; John 3:3,5; 2 Cor. 5:17), all of whom are under a new law, with that law being written in a new place – the heart, not tablets of stone. The consequences of this newness are massive. The 'Israel of God' (Gal. 6:16; see also Rom. 2:28-29; 9:6; Gal. 3:7,29; Phil. 3:3; 1 Pet. 2:9-10) has superseded the nation of Israel, and the law of Christ has superseded the law of Moses.

As evidence that the concept of the new covenant really does pervade the New Testament, think of all the *new* things found in Christ: *new* cloth (Matt. 9:16; Mark 2:21; Luke 5:36); *new* wine in *new* wineskins (Matt. 9:17; Mark 2:22; Luke 5:38; compare Acts 2:13 and Eph. 5:18); *new* doctrine (Acts 17:19); a *new* lump (1 Cor. 5:7); a *new* covenant (Matt. 26:28; Mark 14:24; Luke 22:20; 1 Cor. 11:25, 2 Cor. 3:6; Heb. 8:8,13; 9:15; 12:24) or *new* testament (Heb. 9:15, AV); the believer is a *new* creation (2 Cor. 5:17; Gal. 6:15), a *new*born babe (1 Pet. 2:2), a *new* man (Eph. 2:15; 4:24; Col. 3:10); he comes to God in a *new* and living way (Heb. 10:20), keeping a *new* commandment (John 13:34; 1 John 2:8) in *new*ness of life (Rom. 6:4) and *new*ness of heart and spirit or Spirit (Ezek. 11:19; 36:26; Rom. 7:6), having a *new* name (Isa. 62:2; Rev. 2:17; 3:12), singing a *new* song (Rev. 5:9; 14:3); Christ has now made all things *new* (2 Cor. 5:17; Rev. 21:5), and will do so especially in eternity, where the saints will dwell in the *new* heavens and the *new* earth in the *new* Jerusalem (2 Pet. 3:13; Rev. 3:12; 21:1-2,5)... Think of all the *old* things put away by Christ: the *old* covenant has been abolished (Heb. 8:13), *old* things are gone (2 Cor. 5:17); for the believer, the *old* man has gone (Rom. 6:6) with his *old* sins (2 Pet. 1:9); the believer no longer lives in the *old* way (Eph. 4:22-23; Col. 3:9), serving God with the *old* leaven (1 Cor. 5:7-8). The *old* cloth and *old* wine have had their day (Matt. 9:16-17; Mark 2:21-22; Luke 5:36-38)... Again, think of all which is conjured up by the lovely word *former*; the believer can talk about the passing away of

*The Fundamental Point*

*former* things including his *former* conduct or way of life
(Eph. 4:22), his *former* lusts (1 Pet. 1:14); indeed, he looks
forward to the time when all the *former* things (Rev. 21:4)
will be done away with. Unbelievers have no *former* – and
therefore no *new* – experience. Such belongs entirely and
only to those who are in the *new* covenant, to those who
have been taken out of the *former* covenant. Similarly with
*no longer* (Isa. 62:4)... Reader, I have put these passages
before you to point out how much the doctrine of the new
covenant permeates the New Testament. In truth, it
dominates it. 'Newness' is *the* concept, not surprisingly,
since we are, after all, talking about the *New* Testament, the
age of the '*new* testament', the '*new* covenant'. And it is the
very 'newness' of the new covenant, and the weight which
Scripture gives to this newness, which makes it utterly
incongruous to regard the law of the old covenant as the
perfect rule of life for believers. How can it be? After all,
believers are children of the *new* covenant! All things have
become new (2 Cor. 5:17). *All* things! And this negates the
idea that the law of Christ is not a new law but is the old law
of Moses. But a new law is precisely what it is! A new
commandment Christ gave us (John 13:34). A new law for a
new people, with new promises for that new people.

Scripture teaches that while the two Testaments are
strictly continuous (apart from the 400 year gap), the two
covenants – the old and the new – are radically different,
being even contrasted in Scripture. The one, the Mosaic
covenant, the old covenant, was the covenant of the flesh,
outward, a shadow, ineffective, condemning, killing, a
covenant of death, a temporary covenant for Israel which
was fulfilled by Christ and abolished because it was weak
and useless. The other covenant, the new covenant, is
superior in that it is spiritual, of the Spirit, inward, real (not
shadow) and effective, saving and permanent. The
fundamental disjoint of the two covenants is vital. See John
1:17; Romans 8:3; 10:4; 2 Corinthians 3:6-11; Galatians
3:19; Hebrews 7:12,18,22,28; 8:7-13. No amount of use of
the conjuring trick of the tripartite division of the law

37

(Aquinas *via* Calvin) will evade this.[12] No! I am not advocating what is commonly known as 'dispensationalism'. Nor am I guilty of Marcionism.[13]

So what?

Is that your response? Really? This fundamental point – the contrast in the two covenants – dominates this discussion. And when I say 'discussion', I am not thinking in terms of a mere debate, with no practical consequence. Ignorance of the distinction, the contrast, between the two covenants, leads to all kinds of trouble. In particular, if we forget the contrast between the two covenants, we will be prone to make the puerile mistake of taking promises which applied to Israel in a covenant which was uniquely theirs, a covenant long since rendered obsolete, and have the audacity to 'claim them for ourselves'. This is not only arrogant, it is foolish, and, as I have observed, leads many believers into dreadful – literally speaking – experiences of anguish, self-doubt and torment, grievous experiences which can blight their lives for decades. What is more, when preachers address their hearers on this basis, they should not be surprised if some at least go away with the idea that salvation is by works. After all, they are only playing out the role of unregenerate Israel acting under the terms of the old covenant, 'do and live' being its essence (Lev. 18:5; Rom. 9:33 – 10:5; Gal. 3:10-12).

John Bunyan hit the nail on the head when he declared:

> The reason why souls are deceived by [the devil]... is because they are not able to distinguish between the law and the gospel.[14]

---

[12] See my *Christ Is All*; *Believers*.

[13] In the 2nd century, Marcion rejected the Old Testament and what he saw as the God of the Old Testament. He limited the Bible almost entirely to Paul's letters. To play fair with Marcion, however, we can only construct his views through the writings of his opponents, especially Tertullian.

[14] Bunyan: *Some Gospel Truths Opened*.

Now there is one thing which, for want of, most people do miscarry in a very sad manner; and that is because they are not able to distinguish between the nature of the law and the gospel. O, people, people, your being blinded here as to the knowledge of this [contrast] is one great cause of the ruining of many. As Paul says: 'While Moses is read' – or while the law is opened[13] – 'the veil is upon their heart' (2 Cor. 3:15); that is, the veil of ignorance is still upon their hearts, so that they cannot discern either the nature of the law or the nature of the gospel, they being so dark and blind in their minds – as you may see, if you compare [2 Corinthians 3:15][16] with 2 Corinthians 4:3-4. And truly I am confident that were you but well examined, I am convinced[17] many of you would be found so ignorant that you would not be able to give a word of right answer concerning either the law or the gospel.[18]

He went on, rightly lamenting that many (perhaps most) never even think about the covenants:

No, my friends, if[19] one should ask you what time you spend, what pains you take to the end you may understand the nature and difference of these two covenants, would you not say, if you should speak the truth, that you did not so much as even think about[20] whether there were two or more? Would you not say: 'I did not think of covenants, or study the nature of them.[21]

If that is your response, reader, then do not be surprised if you end up in a mess over the promises of the old covenant! And much else. C.H.Spurgeon:

I am persuaded that most of the mistakes which men make concerning the doctrines of Scripture are based upon

---

[15] Bunyan had 'discovered'.

[16] Bunyan had 'it'.

[17] Bunyan had 'I doubt'. There must be a typo here. Bunyan surely meant 'I doubt not'.

[18] Bunyan: *The Doctrine of the Law and Grace Unfolded.*

[19] Bunyan had 'set the case'.

[20] Bunyan had 'regard'.

[21] Bunyan: *The Doctrine of the Law and Grace Unfolded.*

fundamental errors with regard to the covenants of law and of grace.[22]

Let me give an example or two from history to illustrate what I am saying.

---

[22] C.H.Spurgeon sermon number 3326.

# Examples from History

In this chapter I want to show from history what can happen when believers fail to maintain the contrast between the two covenants, the old and the new. I do this to stress the point that what we are discussing is not an academic nicety, a theological peccadillo, one which has no practical consequence. Confusing the covenants, failing to distinguish between them, carries a high price tag.

Now while by no stretch of the imagination could the Puritans be accused of advocating the prosperity gospel, nevertheless many of them made the fundamental mistake of that teaching;[23] that is, they confused the two covenants, making a hybrid out of what the Bible clearly contrasts. Let me explain.

As I have argued, God has no special earthly nation now; the church is his nation (1 Pet. 2:9). 'There is neither Jew nor Greek' (Gal. 3:28). The Christian's 'citizenship is in heaven' (Phil. 3:20). Great Britain is not a Christian country. There is no such thing; there never has been; there never will be. That kind of talk is the foolish twang of Constantine, not the language of the New Testament. America is not God's own country. England is not the church, it was not the church in the 1640s, it never will be. The same goes for Scotland, Ulster and all the rest. But good men in 1640 thought England was the church or in some way the nation of God, and they acted upon the idea. And look where it got them. We cannot move from the old to the new covenant in this high-handed fashion, taking old-covenant promises and applying them to a nation, a church or to believers individually, without paying a heavy price for our foolishness. But this is a price that many Puritans paid, and caused many others to pay.

---

[23] See my *Battle* pp408-413.

In doing this, the 17th century was echoing the 16th. Richard Fitz had thought of England as favoured Israel; while King Edward VI, more than a decade before Fitz, had regarded the English as the chosen people of God. John Aylmer had taught that 'God is English'! Elizabethan Presbyterians like Thomas Cartwright had asserted that God was in covenant with the people by giving 'the seals... to our assemblies in England'. There was 'a virtual covenant... set up between God and England', he said. John Knox raised his voice similarly for Scotland. John Field had claimed that God had given himself to the English as a people – and not only to the elect within the nation. Following hard upon their predecessors' heels, the Puritans of the 17th century declared openly that God had made the English his elect. John Milton could say God's usual practice was to make his will known 'first to his Englishmen'. To the Puritans, England was the most favoured nation on earth, the very Israel of God. Many Scots, likewise, were persuaded that God was with them as a people. As Samuel Rutherford put it: 'Now, O Scotland, God be thanked, thy name is in the Bible'; taking the place of Israel, he meant. It was all a huge misunderstanding. And very costly.

Nor has it died. For instance, this kind of confusion came to the fore during the fiftieth anniversary of the D-day landings of June, 1944. Let me say at once that it was right and proper for the Allies to wage war against Nazi Germany. The defeat of Hitler and the destruction of his indescribably evil Reich was a noble end. Those who gave their lives in that war died in a worthy cause, and we who have lived to enjoy the liberty they fought for must be grateful to those who suffered, and continue to suffer. We ought ever to have a sense of debt to those who gave so much. Nor must we ever forget those who died for our freedom. All this is utterly self-evident.

But when a passage is read from Bunyan's *Pilgrim's Progress*, speaking of all the trumpets sounding on the other side as Mr Valiant-for-Truth passed over, and it is made to apply to the soldiers who fell in the war – that is most improper. Nevertheless, this is the very thing which happened in the commemorations, and it gave a totally false picture. Those soldiers were not fighting for Christianity; or if they were it was a gross misunderstanding of what Christianity is, and how it is established. The war was a political affair. Allied forces did not fight to establish the church. The combatants were not Christian soldiers, though some think they were. Winston Churchill was one such; he chose the hymn 'Onward, Christian Soldiers' for the Sunday service on board the *Prince of Wales* when he met Franklin D.Roosevelt, and the pulpit was draped with the Union Jack and the Stars and Stripes, he recorded. He, along with all the men, was deeply moved by the experience, he said. But the premise was utterly at fault. Neither the British nor American forces were made up of Christian soldiers. Nor were those who fell in the war saved because they died in a noble cause. This episode is an illustration of just how sadly politics and religion,[24] preaching and war, can get mixed up when well-meaning people become muddled in their thinking over the covenants. And the confusion brings tragic consequences in its wake.

Of course, it is perfectly clear that Israel in the Old Testament did advance its cause by war, the defeat of other nations and the subjugation of its enemies. Religion and politics, war and prophecy were very much united in those days, inasmuch as the old covenant was an external system, couched in material, earthly terms. Things are very different in the New Testament. Where is the New Testament justification for the use of force and political intrigue as the means of spiritual reform? There is none. The old covenant has been abolished in Christ; the new has come (John 1:17;

---

[24] In fact, as he made clear in his war memoirs, Churchill deliberately, and with great attention to detail, orchestrated the entire 'event' – hymns, seating, flags, the lot – to get it captured on film with an eye to drawing America ever closer to entering the war. It was a classic example of a politician using Christendom – prostituting the gospel – to further his own ends. Worthy though that purpose was, it did not justify the abuse.

Rom. 5:20 – 8:4; 2 Cor. 3:5-16; Eph. 2:11-22; Heb. 7:11 – 10:25). Christians must act in the light of this.

Christians, though well-intentioned, often forget the distinction between the two covenants. They disregard the contrast between Christ and Caesar (Matt. 22:21). They confuse the government of Israel of old with our present-day Parliamentary system. They entangle the State and the church. They forget that the kingdom of God is advanced by preaching the gospel, not by enforcing laws. Have they never read that even the law of God itself could not save men? 'For what the law could not do in that it was weak through the flesh, God did by sending his own Son in the likeness of sinful flesh, on account of sin' (Rom. 8:3).

In short, we must always distinguish between Christendom and biblical Christianity. Christendom is an abomination which has wrought eternal ruin for millions. It is doing so even as I write and as you read this. Far more could be said. And in other works I have said some of it – see my *Battle for the Church 1517-1644*; *Infant Baptism Tested*; *The Pastor: Does He Exist?*; *Letting Loose a Gadfly: Edward Miall Speaks Today*; *Deceit in Death: Christendom in the Raw: 'Christian' Last Rites for Unbelievers*. See also my 'Preparationism in New England'.

But it is not just a matter of history – in the sense of mere facts and dates and such like. Remember, we are talking about – and should be thinking about – real men, real women and real children who lived and died under regimes based on principles drawn, not from Scripture and the new covenant, but from the Fathers, who went to the old covenant, and invented that monstrosity, Christendom. All this played into the medieval Roman Church, thence to the magisterial Reformers, the Puritans and so on. The enforcement by the State of what was considered true religion, coupled with infant baptism, led to two things at least. It led to horrendous suffering for those who refused to accept this dogma but were determined to hold to the new covenant, whatever the cost. And it also led to the eternal damnation of a countless number who thought conformity to the prescribed religion meant they were right with God.

And all this has contemporary resonance. And how! Those in the UK or USA or wherever who flirt with the State and the production of 'a Christian nation' are playing with fire. To change the figure, if they get their way they will set up a monster, a monster which will certainly devour dissidents, those who will not submit to such a Babylon but quit it in accordance with apostolic command (2 Cor. 6:14 – 7:1). But not only that. Those who invent such a monster – or dream of it – should always bear in mind that it will eventually come back to bite those who toy with it.

Finally, never forget the millions who are deceived, even at this very moment – deceived into thinking that being religious, doing good works, or engaging in ritual, or whatever, is what makes them right with God. Think of that! Think of them!

# *Boasting?*

Having settled the basic point, having established (or reminded ourselves) that the promises of the old covenant belonged to Israel, and only Israel, in the days of the old covenant, we can now go further. The promises in question are unreservedly conditional, heavily conditional. There is a decided *if* about them. If Israel met the conditions, then God would fulfil the promise. If Israel failed to meet the conditions, Israel would not receive the blessing; indeed, the people would suffer God's curse. God, on occasion, might show extraordinary mercy to Israel, but the promises we are talking about were all heavily dependent on fulfilling the conditions.

Take this:

> When I shut up the heavens so that there is no rain, or command the locust to devour the land, or send pestilence among my people, if my people who are called by my name humble themselves, and pray and seek my face and turn from their wicked ways, then I will hear from heaven and will forgive their sin and heal their land (2 Chron. 7:13-14).

And this:

> 'Bring the full tithe into the storehouse, that there may be food in my house. And thereby put me to the test', says the LORD of hosts, 'if I will not open the windows of heaven for you and pour down for you a blessing until there is no more need. I will rebuke the devourer for you, so that it will not destroy the fruits of your soil, and your vine in the field shall not fail to bear', says the LORD of hosts. 'Then all nations will call you blessed, for you will be a land of delight', says the LORD of hosts (Mal. 3:10-12).

The conditional nature of the promises is patent. Take this:

> The LORD... heals all your diseases (Ps. 103:2-3).

But do not forget the condition:

> The steadfast love of the LORD is from everlasting to everlasting on those who fear him, and his righteousness to children's children, to those who keep his covenant and remember to do his commandments (Ps. 103:17-18).

Naturally, inevitably, it follows that if an Israelite met the conditions and so received the blessing, he had grounds for boasting. 'I have met the conditions; I have claimed the promise. I have received what God promised; *ergo*, I must have met the conditions. I claim it; I assert it'. The same goes for the nation. Call it by any other name, and it is still boasting. Even if the element of pride is absent, nevertheless the basic truth still stands; obedience has brought its reward. And this must inevitably lead to an element of self-congratulation, a singing of one's own praise. We know that this is what happened. This is the context in which the psalmist made his appeal to God:

> Judge me, O LORD, according to my righteousness and according to the integrity that is in me (Ps. 7:8).

It is the context in which the psalmist was able to declare that the Lord had kept his word to him, and did so because he had met the conditions God had spelled out:

> The LORD dealt with me according to my righteousness; according to the cleanness of my hands he rewarded me. For I have kept the ways of the LORD, and have not wickedly departed from my God. For all his rules [just decrees] were before me, and his statutes I did not put away from me. I was blameless before him, and I kept myself from my guilt. So the LORD has rewarded me according to my righteousness, according to the cleanness of my hands in his sight (Ps. 18:20-24).

In short, under the old covenant Israel could be certain that:

> ...the LORD rewards every man for his righteousness and his faithfulness (1 Sam. 26:23).

> [God] will render to a man according to his work (Ps. 62:12).

But this of course was in the days of the old covenant. Nevertheless, boasting was a very real possibility, a probable outcome of that covenant and its promises. It seem to me that passages such as Isaiah 48:2; Micah 3:11; John 5:39,45; 8:41; 9:28 play into this.

It is easy to see how those upon whom the sun was shining, those upon whom God was smiling, could attribute this to their obedience, and how they could dismiss those who were suffering – dismiss them as those suffering because of their disobedience. It was all a question of justice: obey, and be blessed; disobey, and suffer for it. In other words, because blessing was earned by obedience, those who were blessed had something to boast about – both the blessing and their obedience that merited it.

Now, we are left in no doubt that such a spirit is utterly out of place in the new covenant:

> Then what becomes of our boasting? It is excluded. By what kind of law? By a law of works? No, but by the law of faith (Rom. 3:27).

> ...so that no human being might boast in the presence of God (1 Cor. 1:29).

> No one may boast (Eph. 2:9).

But, even in the days of the new covenant, many Jews – it seemed to be a general characteristic of the nation – still defiantly breathing the atmosphere of the old covenant, thought they could boast. And so they did! Hear them:

> You call yourself a Jew and rely on the law and boast in God... You... boast in the law (Rom. 2:17,23).

Paul immediately stamped on it. He certainly did all he could to disabuse the Jews (and believers, of course) of any such notion, and he lost no time about it. He was adamant that it is an absolute essential of the new covenant that boasting is excluded; there is no room or cause for it whatsoever:

> If Abraham was justified by works, he has something to boast about (Rom. 4:2).

49

Of course, even in the days of the old covenant, spiritual men and women knew this, and said as much:

> Ascribe to the LORD, O heavenly beings, ascribe to the LORD glory and strength. Ascribe to the LORD the glory due to his name (Ps. 29:1-2).

> Ascribe to the LORD, O families of the peoples, ascribe to the LORD glory and strength! Ascribe to the LORD the glory due to his name (Ps. 96:7-8).

> Not to us, O LORD, not to us, but to your name give glory (Ps. 115:1).

But they were living virtually in the new covenant.[25]

Coming to the question in hand: boasting, crowing, must be an inevitable outcome of the prosperity gospel. Those who are blessed are blessed because they are superior believers. They receive God's blessing because they have met the conditions attached to the promise. Those who suffer are second class; they fail to come up to scratch. There is no baulking these facts.

As I have said, the prosperity gospel also tends – to put it no stronger – to salvation by works. It will be almost impossible for those who listen to prosperity-gospel teachers to distinguish, on the one hand, the promise of eternal life, salvation and justification by faith from, on the other hand, the promise of health and wealth. Both – health and eternal happiness – will come if they meet the conditions and claim the promise. It is all a question of merit. They have merited their wealth and health; they have merited their eternal salvation.

But this is not the only thing to bear in mind. What about the other side of the coin? Boasting is one thing. But what about disappointment? Will prosperity-gospel teachers be willing to admit their failures? In the cases I mentioned in the chapter 'The Issue', why couldn't the people involved admit the lack of cure, acknowledging it must have been some

---

[25] See my *Psalm 119*; *Believers*; *Christ Is All*.

spiritual defect in the wife, some failure in the brother, or some coming short by the onlookers who were praying? Why not accept the fact that because they had failed in some way, God handed down the curse? They boast of the blessing for obedience. Why stop there? Why not play 100% fair with Scripture and admit that the lack of blessing, the lack of a positive answer to the prayer, must have been caused by some failure on their part? Why not admit their disobedience? In talking like this, I am, I hope it goes without saying, speaking in line with what might be called 'the terms of engagement' of the prosperity gospel.

The right thing to do, of course, is for prosperity gospellers to drop their system, show a biblical spirit, stop claiming promises in their cavalier way, and recognise the sovereignty of God in all the events (whether seemingly good or bad) of an individual's life from birth to death. I am thinking of Job,[26] who, when he got news of the disasters beginning to pour in upon him, responded with consummate faith and resignation to the will of God, declaring:

> Naked I came from my mother's womb, and naked shall I return. The Lord gave, and the Lord has taken away; blessed be the name of the Lord (Job 1:21).

And God honoured him for his stance:

> In all this Job did not sin or charge God with wrong (Job 1:22).

It was no flash in the pan on Job's part. As things got even worse, Job's wife joined in the attack upon the good man:

> Then his wife said to him: 'Do you still hold fast your integrity? Curse God and die' (Job 2:9).

Nevertheless, Job held on. He replied:

---

[26] And not only Job. See also Ex. 4:11; Hannah's song or prayer of praise in 1 Sam. 2:1-10; Ps. 75:7.

You speak as one of the foolish women would speak. Shall we receive good from God, and shall we not receive evil? (Job 2:10).

God's verdict? Just this:

In all this Job did not sin with his lips (Job 2:10).

Reliance on, and submission to, the sovereignty of God, not boasting about their ability to have constant success in 'claiming the promise', is the right spirit for believers. Failing in this regard, the property gospellers, with what I can only call their arrogance, get very close to falling foul of James' rebuke:

Come now, you who say: 'Today or tomorrow we will go into such and such a town and spend a year there and trade and make a profit' – yet you do not know what tomorrow will bring. What is your life? For you are a mist that appears for a little time and then vanishes. Instead you ought to say: 'If the Lord wills, we will live and do this or that'. As it is, you boast in your arrogance. All such boasting is evil (Jas. 4:13-16).

On the wider front, the gospel is not all in the major key – blessing. Far from it! The minor key also plays its vital part in the gospel harmony. Christ did not fail to spell out both blessing and curse. Take John 3. See how clear he was on the love of God in the salvation of those who trust him (John 3:15-18), but equally clear on the wrath of God for those who refuse (John 3:15-19,36).

Similarly, the life of the believer is not all sunshine. Lowering clouds cover his sky at times, clouds which do not always lift. But he knows that all is disposed by God in his sovereignty for the believer's good.[27] We need to learn this and 'inwardly digest' it. As John Berridge's biblically-sweet words remind us, we can even sing about it:

> *How watchful is the loving Lord,*
> *How sweet his providential word,*
> *To children that believe!*

---

[27] I will return to this in the chapter 'Objections'.

*Boasting?*

*Your very hairs are numbered all;*
*Not one by force or chance can fall*
*Without your Father's leave.*

*Why should I fear when guarded so,*
*Or shrink to meet a deadly foe?*
*His mouth is held with bit;*
*I need not dread his utmost spite,*
*Nor can he bark, nor can he bite,*
*Unless the Lord permit.*

*No cross or bliss, no loss or gain,*
*No health nor sickness, ease nor pain,*
*Can give themselves a birth;*
*The Lord so rules by his command,*
*Nor good nor ill can stir a hand,*
*Unless he send them forth.*

*Since thou so kind and watchful art,*
*To guard my head and guard my heart,*
*And guard my very hair,*
*Teach me with child-like mind to sit,*
*And sing at my dear Saviour's feet,*
*Without distrust or fear.*

*So, like a pilgrim, let me wait,*
*Contented well in every state,*
*Till all my warfare ends;*
*Live in a calm and cheerful mood,*
*And find that all things work for good,*
*Which Jesus kindly sends.*

Why won't the prosperity gospellers face up to what the Bible teaches about this and the believer's response to it? How much spiritual benefit they lose, and how much emotional anguish they cause, with their misguided emphasis upon the material, the here and now, and their boast of unmitigated happiness all the way!

In the following chapter, I will explore this a little more, starting with the old covenant.

# Not All Blessing!

Prosperity gospellers like to talk about the promised blessings which – they claim – are always received by them. But blessing in the old covenant was only half the story. Now a half truth is a lie. The old covenant was rich with blessings promised to Israel, certainly, but, alongside those promises, God issued warnings and attendant curses for failure. If Israel kept the covenant and its law, well and good, but when Israel broke the covenant and transgressed the law, disaster stared them in the face. And the history of Israel, beginning with the golden calf at Sinai, is replete with example after example of it. I might almost say that the history of Israel is a record of disobedience and consequent judgment. There were some high spots, but the general course was downward, having started at a low point.

Prosperity-gospel teachers like to talk about the promises. What about the curses?

Take the promises quoted earlier.

Let us start with God's word to Israel through Malachi:

> 'Bring the full tithe into the storehouse, that there may be food in my house. And thereby put me to the test', says the LORD of hosts, 'if I will not open the windows of heaven for you and pour down for you a blessing until there is no more need. I will rebuke the devourer for you, so that it will not destroy the fruits of your soil, and your vine in the field shall not fail to bear', says the LORD of hosts. 'Then all nations will call you blessed, for you will be a land of delight', says the LORD of hosts (Mal. 3:10-12).

What caused the drought, the dearth, the famine in the first place? God through Malachi again:

> 'From the days of your fathers you have turned aside from my statutes and have not kept them. Return to me, and I will return to you', says the LORD of hosts. 'But you say: "How shall we return?" Will a man rob God? Yet you are

robbing me. But you say: "How have we robbed you?" In your tithes and contributions. You are cursed with a curse, for you are robbing me, the whole nation of you' (Mal. 3:7-9).

In other words, God, addressing Israel, was telling them that if they stopped sinning – ceased their transgression of his covenant and its law – and if they returned to him, returned to his covenant and law, obeyed him in his law, then he would bless them, bless them materially, and with abundance. If they did not... the curse would remain.

Now for 2 Chronicles. Yes, God assured Solomon that, if Israel returned to him, he would remove the curse of drought from them and their land:

> When I shut up the heavens so that there is no rain, or command the locust to devour the land, or send pestilence among my people, if my people who are called by my name humble themselves, and pray and seek my face and turn from their wicked ways, then I will hear from heaven and will forgive their sin and heal their land (2 Chron. 7:13-14).

This is the point. God was responding to Solomon's prayer. Read that prayer and see:

> If a man sins against his neighbour and is made to take an oath and comes and swears his oath before your altar in this house, then hear from heaven and act and judge your servants, repaying the guilty by bringing his conduct on his own head, and vindicating the righteous by rewarding him according to his righteousness.
> If your people Israel are defeated before the enemy because they have sinned against you, and they turn again and acknowledge your name and pray and plead with you in this house, then hear from heaven and forgive the sin of your people Israel and bring them again to the land that you gave to them and to their fathers.
> When heaven is shut up and there is no rain because they have sinned against you, if they pray toward this place and acknowledge your name and turn from their sin, when you afflict them, then hear in heaven and forgive the sin of your servants, your people Israel, when you teach them the good way in which they should walk, and grant rain upon your

land, which you have given to your people as an inheritance.
If there is famine in the land, if there is pestilence or blight or mildew or locust or caterpillar, if their enemies besiege them in the land at their gates, whatever plague, whatever sickness there is... (2 Chron. 6:22-28).

This, of course, all stemmed from the giving of the covenant through Moses at Sinai, which covenant was restated just as Israel was preparing to enter the land of promise. At that time, God spelled out, in the fullest detail, his terms in that covenant – its blessings and its curses, its curses and its blessings. God used Moses to lay all this on the line for Israel just before they reached the promised land, after their years under God's judgment in the wilderness (Deut. 26:16 – 30:20). In the plains of Moab, God spelled it out for Israel. When you get to the land, said God, if you disobey my law then unmitigated material curses will fall upon you; obey my law, and unmitigated material blessings will be yours. Listen to the closing summary Moses issued to Israel:

See, I have set before you today life and good, death and evil. If you obey the commandments of the LORD your God that I command you today, by loving the LORD your God, by walking in his ways, and by keeping his commandments and his statutes and his rules [just decrees], then you shall live and multiply, and the LORD your God will bless you in the land that you are entering to take possession of it. But if your heart turns away, and you will not hear, but are drawn away to worship other gods and serve them, I declare to you today, that you shall surely perish. You shall not live long in the land that you are going over the Jordan to enter and possess. I call heaven and earth to witness against you today, that I have set before you life and death, blessing and curse. Therefore choose life, that you and your offspring may live, loving the LORD your God, obeying his voice and holding fast to him, for he is your life and length of days, that you may dwell in the land that the LORD swore to your fathers, to Abraham, to Isaac, and to Jacob, to give them (Deut. 30:15-20).

Do not miss the point. Read the curses (Deut. 27:9-26) followed by the blessings, and in that order (Deut. 28:1-14). After a clear warning, God repeated it all again, doing so with a very heavy emphasis on the curses (Deut. 28:15-68; 30:1ff).

Note also the reinforcement which followed hard upon the heels of that:

> And the LORD said to Moses: 'Behold, the days approach when you must die. Call Joshua and present yourselves in the tent of meeting, that I may commission him'.
> And Moses and Joshua went and presented themselves in the tent of meeting. And the LORD appeared in the tent in a pillar of cloud. And the pillar of cloud stood over the entrance of the tent. And the LORD said to Moses: 'Behold, you are about to lie down with your fathers. Then this people will rise and whore after the foreign gods among them in the land that they are entering, and they will forsake me and break my covenant that I have made with them. Then my anger will be kindled against them in that day, and I will forsake them and hide my face from them, and they will be devoured. And many evils and troubles will come upon them, so that they will say in that day: "Have not these evils come upon us because our God is not among us?" And I will surely hide my face in that day because of all the evil that they have done, because they have turned to other gods. Now therefore write this song and teach it to the people of Israel. Put it in their mouths, that this song may be a witness for me against the people of Israel. For when I have brought them into the land flowing with milk and honey, which I swore to give to their fathers, and they have eaten and are full and grown fat, they will turn to other gods and serve them, and despise me and break my covenant. And when many evils and troubles have come upon them, this song shall confront them as a witness (for it will live unforgotten in the mouths of their offspring). For I know what they are inclined to do even today, before I have brought them into the land that I swore to give them'.
> So Moses wrote this song the same day and taught it to the people of Israel (Deut. 31:14-22).

And so on...

And when Israel entered the land, the people had to inscribe the curses on one rock on Mount Ebal, and the blessings on another (Deut. 27:1-4,12-14).

And this is the context for the promises in 2 Chronicles and Malachi. It is also the context in which the psalmist made his appeal to God in Psalm: 7:8 and Psalm 18:20-24. See also the extracts from 1 Samuel 26:23 and Psalm 62:12.

As for Solomon and his wonderful prayer, look at the mess he made of his life! How deeply and how quickly did he ruin himself by transgression of the covenant and breaking God's law! And how rapidly after his death did Israel fall apart, fall beyond recovery! The glory days for Israel never returned – no, not even under Ezra and Nehemiah and the post-exile prophets. It is not without significance that the closing word of the Old Testament is 'curse' or its equivalent:

> Behold, I will send you Elijah the prophet before the great and awesome day of the LORD comes. And he will turn the hearts of fathers to their children and the hearts of children to their fathers, lest I come and strike the land with a decree of utter destruction (Mal. 4:5-6).

Putting all this together, we can see that the prosperity-gospel teachers are in danger – to put it no stronger – of giving the impression that they are being highly selective. They like the promises, but are they as keen on the curses? Think of the injustice of claiming only the 'pleasant' bits of the promises, and ignoring the conditions and, following their failure to meet those conditions, having to suffer the curses. Above all, think of doing this with a covenant that was meant for Israel only, a covenant which has been fulfilled and thus rendered obsolete by Christ! God is not 'partial' (Deut. 10:17-18). Israel was never allowed to treat the law and the promises as a menu from which to make a selection (Deut. 1:17; Mal. 2:9). They were never given authority to plump for the 'goodies' and leave the 'nasty' bits. For believers today to do this with a covenant which is not theirs is, or ought to be, unthinkable. Such irresponsible audacity won't wash. We are, after all, talking about

Scripture. And this cavalier reading and consequent application of Scripture is offensive as well as foolish.

But there is something else.

# Simplistic!

I closed the previous chapter by saying that prosperity-gospel way of reading and applying Scripture is cavalier, and, as such, it is offensive as well as foolish. I also observed that there is more to be said. The prosperity gospel is simplistic and naïve. Let me explain.

Spiritual men in the days of the old covenant had their heads screwed on. Even in the days of the promises in question, they realised there was more to life than the prosperity gospellers like to think. Take this from the psalmist:

> Truly God is good to Israel, to those who are pure in heart.

Well, what's remarkable about that? Typical old-covenant teaching, is it not? Of course! But look how the psalmist went on:

> But as for me, my feet had almost stumbled, my steps had nearly slipped. For I was envious of the arrogant when I saw the prosperity of the wicked. For they have no pangs until death; their bodies are fat and sleek. They are not in trouble as others are; they are not stricken like the rest of mankind. Therefore pride is their necklace; violence covers them as a garment. Their eyes swell out through fatness; their hearts overflow with follies. They scoff and speak with malice; loftily they threaten oppression. They set their mouths against the heavens, and their tongue struts through the earth. Therefore his people turn back to them, and find no fault in them. And they say: 'How can God know? Is there knowledge in the Most High?' Behold, these are the wicked; always at ease, they increase in riches. All in vain have I kept my heart clean and washed my hands in innocence. For all the day long I have been stricken and rebuked every morning. If I had said: 'I will speak thus', I would have betrayed the generation of your children. But when I thought how to understand this, it seemed to me a wearisome task, until I went into the sanctuary of God; then I discerned their end (Ps. 73:1-17).

Job, in the days before the giving of the Mosaic covenant, found it so:

> I, who called to God and he answered me, a just and blameless man, am a laughingstock. In the thought of one who is at ease there is contempt for misfortune; it is ready for those whose feet slip. The tents of robbers are at peace, and those who provoke God are secure, who bring their god in their hand (Job 12:4-6).

> Why do the wicked live, reach old age, and grow mighty in power? Their offspring are established in their presence, and their descendants before their eyes. Their houses are safe from fear, and no rod of God is upon them. Their bull breeds without fail; their cow calves and does not miscarry. They send out their little boys like a flock, and their children dance. They sing to the tambourine and the lyre and rejoice to the sound of the pipe. They spend their days in prosperity, and in peace they go down to Sheol. They say to God: 'Depart from us! We do not desire the knowledge of your ways. What is the Almighty, that we should serve him? And what profit do we get if we pray to him?' Behold, is not their prosperity in their hand? The counsel of the wicked is far from me (Job 21:7-16).

Job admitted this was not the whole story, as the context makes clear. But he recognised the issue. He knew things were far from simple.

The psalmist had to take himself in hand:

> Fret not yourself over the one who prospers in his way, over the man who carries out evil devices! (Ps. 37:7).

And the sacred teacher knew things were not so straightforward as the prosperity gospellers want to us to think:

> There is a vanity that takes place on earth, that there are righteous people to whom it happens according to the deeds of the wicked, and there are wicked people to whom it happens according to the deeds of the righteous. I said that this also is vanity (Eccles. 8:14).

Jeremiah was another such:

Why does the way of the wicked prosper? Why do all who are treacherous thrive? You plant them, and they take root; they grow and produce fruit; you are near in their mouth and far from their heart (Jer. 12:1-2).

As was Habakkuk:

You who are of purer eyes than to see evil and cannot look at wrong, why do you idly look at traitors and remain silent when the wicked swallows up the man more righteous than he? You make mankind like the fish of the sea, like crawling things that have no ruler. He [that is, the wicked enemy] brings all of them up with a hook; he drags them out with his net; he gathers them in his dragnet; so he rejoices and is glad. Therefore he sacrifices to his net and makes offerings to his dragnet; for by them he lives in luxury, and his food is rich. Is he then to keep on emptying his net and mercilessly killing nations forever? (Hab. 13:13-17

Yes, I know these writers said other things, but they said this much. It shows they had to wrestle with the issue. They were not naïve, doing the impossible, trying to walk with their heads in the sand. They, even in the days of the old covenant and before, knew that life had a bit more to it than the way prosperity gospellers would like. They knew that it was not always easy to fit the circumstances of life with the promises of God! Scripture – whichever covenant we are talking about – always leaves the best of men, those with the clearest brains, the most spiritual insight, floundering. It is yet another illustration of the folly of trying to confine Scripture – the mind of God revealed to us poor mortals – into any template of man's devising, however venerable that template might be by reason of age or tradition.

Clearly, then, prosperity gospellers, covenant theologians, dispensationalists and all the rest, are mistaken. But what is the right approach? What can we learn from these old-covenant promises?

# The Positive

I hope this chapter will make it clear why I chose 'Beyond the Negative' as the title for this book.

While the stress must be laid on the discontinuity of the old and new covenants, this does not mean there is no continuity at all. God is always the same:

> God is not man, that he should lie, or a son of man, that he should change his mind. Has he said, and will he not do it? Or has he spoken, and will he not fulfil it? (Num. 23:19).

> I the LORD do not change (Mal. 3:6).

> [God] the Father of lights, with whom there is no variation or shadow due to change (Jas. 1:17).

Christ is always the same:

> Jesus Christ is the same yesterday and today and forever (Heb. 13:8).

God is unchanging and unchangeable; so is his plan of redemption, decreed in eternity past, worked out in time, culminating in eternity future. The two covenants – the old and the new – are distinct and contrasted, yes – but God's one purpose in the redemption of his elect is unaltered and unalterable. It is only new-covenant theology that really sets this out. Covenant theologians and many dispensationalists fail in this regard.

So what are we to make of this continuity? Especially, what are we to make of the prosperity promises given to Israel under the old covenant? I have delineated what these promises do not mean for us as believers today. We know what we should not take from them. But what do they mean? What should we take from them? What comes over into the new covenant? Surely – surely it must be an absolute given – we should not be content to be negative. True, those promises belonged to an epoch, to a people and a covenant, long rendered obsolete by Christ in accordance with the eternal purpose of God. Even so, being part of the word of God, remaining part of the word of God, they do speak to us as believers today. They must speak to us today. They have a vital message to convey to us. And we are diminished if we do not listen to that message. In addition, if we fail to draw positive lessons from these passages of Scripture, we show that we do not really take 2 Timothy 3:15-16 seriously. Furthermore, we grievously misrepresent new-covenant theology if we do not set out the positives which we can and must draw from the old-covenant promises.

For, let me remind you, when he was writing to Timothy, Paul set out the definitive, guiding – governing – position for every believer throughout this age:

> All Scripture is breathed out by God and profitable for teaching, for reproof, for correction, and for training in righteousness, that the man of God may be complete, equipped for every good work (2 Tim. 3:16-17).

All Scripture, every scripture – yes, even those promises which belonged to Israel in the old, and now-fulfilled, covenant – continue to speak to us today, and are 'profitable' for us. We know how the prosperity gospellers misread these promises. But, granting that we cannot play ducks and drakes with Scripture – simply grabbing these promises out of context – how should we read them? What is right, what is valuable, for us today, living in the liberty of the new covenant in Christ? What principles are laid out for us in these passages?

***The promises played a vital role in the history of redemption revealed by God through covenants.*** Surely this must take pride of place. The old covenant had a very significant role to play in the history of redemption through covenants, even though that covenant was a temporary covenant for a specific people, brought in with a definitive end-date in God's mind. In particular, the old-covenant promises figured prominently in this. So, as we set out the historical revelation of the redemption God decreed in eternity past, the redemption accomplished through the person and work of Christ, and which is now being applied by the sovereign Spirit, we must lay proper stress on this historical role of the Mosaic covenant.[28] In other words, we need to emphasise the historical role the old-covenant promises played in all this. *But this does not mean that we treat them merely as museum pieces.* We do not leave it there.

This opening section I regard as seminal, standing at the head of all I will go on to say in this chapter. I want to go on and develop it, setting out its ramifications in detail, arguing – with reasons – that we must not stop at the negative when dealing with the promises of the old covenant.

*Law is integral to both covenants, the old and the new.* In the old covenant, Israel was under the law of God which was, for that nation, the law of Moses. In the new covenant, believers are under the law of God, which, for the Israel of God, is the law of Christ.

Why do I stress this obvious point? Because the promises we are concerned with are intimately bound up with the concept of law, the Mosaic law. The law set out commandments, and those commandments implied or spelled out conditions which had blessings attached to them, blessings for Israel in that economy. Putting it the other way round, God gave Israel promises, but with conditions attached. We are, of course, talking about the law of Moses.

Consider the fifth of the ten commandments:

> Honour your father and your mother, that your days may be long in the land that the LORD your God is giving you (Ex. 20:12).

Paul is explicit when he quotes this command as a paradigm for believers:

> Honour your father and mother (this is the first commandment with a promise), that it may go well with you and that you may live long in the land (Eph. 6:2-3).

---

[28] See my *Redemption*.

'This [the fifth] is the first commandment with a promise'. In saying this, Paul was clearly indicating that other old-covenant commands also had promises attached to them.

Take the fourth:

> Remember the sabbath day, to keep it holy. Six days you shall labour, and do all your work, but the seventh day is a sabbath to the LORD your God. On it you shall not do any work, you, or your son, or your daughter, your male servant, or your female servant, or your livestock, or the sojourner who is within your gates. For in six days the LORD made heaven and earth, the sea, and all that is in them, and rested on the seventh day. Therefore the LORD blessed the sabbath day and made it holy (Ex. 20:8-11).

Although there was no promise attached to the sabbath command as it was issued to Israel through Moses on Sinai, God certainly promised blessing to his old-covenant people for sabbath keeping:

> If you turn back your foot from the sabbath, from doing your pleasure on my holy day, and call the sabbath a delight and the holy day of the LORD honourable; if you honour it, not going your own ways, or seeking your own pleasure, or talking idly; then you shall take delight in the LORD, and I will make you ride on the heights of the earth; I will feed you with the heritage of Jacob your father, for the mouth of the LORD has spoken (Isa. 58:13-14).

The point I draw from this is to stress that promise and law, law and promise, were intimately connected in the old covenant. I further assert that the same applies in the new covenant. And this positive use of the promises in question must not be missed. It reminds us of a very important principle; promise and command, command and promise, cannot be divorced. We have seen how Paul uses these laws and promises as paradigms – not as direct binding rules – for us as believers in the day of the new covenant. The new covenant has its law and associated promises. This deduction we must draw from the old covenant.

***Obedience is integral to both covenants, the old and the new.*** Under the old covenant, God demanded obedience. Likewise, under the new covenant God demands obedience. Yes, believers have liberty, but this liberty is the freedom and power to show their love to God in Christ by a willing, heart obedience to the law of Christ. Liberty is not licence. As Gordon D.Fee encapsulated it, believers have freedom, but that freedom is not 'freedom *from*, but freedom *to*'.[29] We are talking about the believer and his progressive sanctification. Progressive sanctification is not an option for the believer; it is an absolute essential.[30] The sinner, having been regenerated, immediately on his trusting Christ is, by faith, united to his Redeemer. As a result of his union with Christ, the believer is immediately both justified and positionally sanctified, and begins a life of progressive sanctification.[31] He is at once a saint and is being sanctified (see Heb. 10:10,14; 12:14, for instance). And this progressive sanctification is a life of obedience to the commands of Christ. For the believer, the law of Christ is not advisory; Christ's commands are mandatory.[32]

A great mark of the new covenant is that the child of God, by the inward work of the Spirit, is moved to love and obey the written law of God, the law of Christ as revealed in the Scriptures (Ezek. 11:20; 36:27); love followed by obedience, obedience prompted by love, please note. It is the one who loves Christ that keeps his commandments (Matt. 28:18-10; John 12:47 – 16:33). Jesus makes it an absolute *sine qua non* (that is, essential) that the child of God obeys Christ's law. Let me quote the relevant scriptures in John 12:47 – 16:33. First, the one overall commandment:

---

[29] Gordon D.Fee: *God's Empowering Presence: The Holy Spirit in the Letters of Paul*, Hendrickson Publishers, Peabody, Massachusetts, 1994, pp313-314.
[30] See my 'Progressive Sanctification: A Matter of Eternal Life or Death'.
[31] See my *Eternal*; *Fivefold*; *Positional*.
[32] See my *Believers*; *Liberty*.

> A new commandment I give to you, that you love one another: just as I have loved you, you also are to love one another (John 13:34).

This, of course, is an envelope in which are found all the other countless imperatives of the new covenant; that is, Christ's law. For a start, we have the series of commandments within Christ's own discourse:

> You call me Teacher and Lord, and you are right, for so I am. If I then, your Lord and Teacher, have washed your feet, you also ought to wash one another's feet. For I have given you an example, that you also should do just as I have done to you... If you love me, you will keep my commandments... Whoever has my commandments and keeps them, he it is who loves me... Whoever does not love me does not keep my words. And the word that you hear is not mine but the Father's who sent me... Abide in me... If you keep my commandments, you will abide in my love, just as I have kept my Father's commandments and abide in his love. These things I have spoken to you, that my joy may be in you, and that your joy may be full. This is my commandment, that you love one another as I have loved you. Greater love has no one than this, that someone lay down his life for his friends. You are my friends if you do what I command you... These things I command you, so that you will love one another (John 13:13-15; 14:15,21,24; 15:4,10-14,17).

And now, within this last great discourse, replete as it is with Christ's commandments gathered under the umbrella of his one 'new commandment', we meet the far-reaching promise of the gift and ministry of the Spirit to enable the apostles to complete the task of setting out Christ's law for all his people for all time, to the end of the age:

> These things I have spoken to you while I am still with you. But the Helper, the Holy Spirit, whom the Father will send in my name, he will teach you all things and bring to your remembrance all that I have said to you... When the Helper comes, whom I will send to you from the Father, the Spirit of truth, who proceeds from the Father, he will bear witness about me... I have said all these things to you to keep you

from falling away... I have said these things to you that...
you may remember that I told them to you... I still have
many things to say to you, but you cannot bear them now.
When the Spirit of truth comes, he will guide you into all
the truth, for he will not speak on his own authority, but
whatever he hears he will speak, and he will declare to you
the things that are to come. He will glorify me, for he will
take what is mine and declare it to you. All that the Father
has is mine; therefore I said that he will take what is mine
and declare it to you (John 14:25-26; 15:26; 16:1,4,12-15).

In light of this, it comes as no surprise to read the apostles
insisting on the right to issue commands in the name of
Christ. And what else can this be but 'the law of Christ'?

It could not be clearer: it is both the believer's duty and
privilege that he is under obligation to obey Christ, but he
has the assurance of the inward work of the Spirit to move
and empower him to that obedience. Not, it goes without
saying, that his progressive sanctification will ever be perfect
in this life – hence the adjective 'progressive'. While
Scripture teaches that the believer is justified and
positionally sanctified in Christ, immediately perfect at the
point of faith by virtue of his union with Christ, it makes it
equally explicit that he must live this out in a life of
progressive sanctification, growing in grace and Christ-
likeness. This is not an option; it is essential. However, he
can do this only because he has died to the law and been
united to Christ, being now under new ownership, with a
new Lord, and married to a new husband – Christ. The
believer's progressive sanctification comes through the
power of the Spirit within, the one who gives him a new
heart to love and obey, with determination, the law of Christ
written throughout the Scriptures. I will not argue all this
here, having done so at length in several works.[33]

The believer's motive for progressive sanctification is not
mere duty. Nor is it servile. The motive is love, heartfelt love
– love to God and love to neighbour. The Spirit writes the

[33] See, in particular, my *Believers*; *Liberty*; *Fivefold*; *Positional*;
*Christ Is All*; *Gadfly*.

law of Christ on the believer's heart – 'heart' certainly speaks of love. As Paul put it:

> The one who loves another has fulfilled the law. For the commandments, 'You shall not commit adultery, You shall not murder, You shall not steal, You shall not covet', and any other commandment, are summed up in this word: 'You shall love your neighbour as yourself'. Love does no wrong to a neighbour; therefore love is the fulfilling of the law (Rom. 13:8-10).

> You were called to freedom, brothers. Only do not use your freedom as an opportunity for the flesh, but through love serve one another. For the whole law is fulfilled in one word: 'You shall love your neighbour as yourself' (Gal. 5:13-14).

> By this we know that we have come to know him, if we keep his commandments. Whoever says "I know him" but does not keep his commandments is a liar, and the truth is not in him, but whoever keeps his word, in him truly the love of God is perfected. By this we may know that we are in him: whoever says he abides in him ought to walk in the same way in which he walked (2 John 2:3-6).

> Everyone who believes that Jesus is the Christ has been born of God, and everyone who loves the Father loves whoever has been born of him. By this we know that we love the children of God, when we love God and obey his commandments. For this is the love of God, that we keep his commandments. And his commandments are not burdensome (1 John 5:1-3).

This is why we must not stop at the negative when dealing with the promises of the old covenant. Those promises were tied, unbreakably tied, to commandments in that covenant. The same principle carries over into the new covenant. The believer has to obey Christ's law. And there is a promised blessing in his so-doing:

> If you know these things, blessed are you if you do them (John 13:17).

> Be doers of the word, and not hearers only, deceiving yourselves. For if anyone is a hearer of the word and not a

doer, he is like a man who looks intently at his natural face in a mirror. For he looks at himself and goes away and at once forgets what he was like. But the one who looks into the perfect law, the law of liberty, and perseveres, being no hearer who forgets but a doer who acts, he will be blessed in his doing (Jas. 1:22-25).

While believers do not claim the old-covenant promises by meeting the conditions, nor do they claim new-covenant promises and blessings, they do obey Christ's law because they are forgiven and have been given a new heart, and they are blessed in their obedience.

And this takes us to the next point. The law of Christ is more penetrating than the law of Moses.

***The law of Christ is more penetrating than the law of Moses.*** The Mosaic covenant and the new covenant are very different. While both have law intimately bound up in them, whereas God's law for Israel under the old covenant was the Mosaic law, in the new covenant the law for believers is the law of Christ. Having, in previous works,[34] set this out as fully as I know how, I will say no more here except to add that this is no soft option. The law of Christ is more penetrating than the law of Moses. New-covenant theology is anything but 'woolly' or 'fuzzy', despite what our critics allege.

Why do I say this here? Because it follows on from the previous point. The old covenant had its conditions as the promises made clear. So does the new. I readily agree – and have argued – that the new covenant really is a new covenant. Even so, it does have penetrating conditions. Indeed, as I have shown in previous works, the law of Christ is more penetrating than the law of Moses. The promises remind us of this fact.

And now for a very important point. Not only is this point important; it is highly contested. One of the reasons which

---

[34] See, for instance, my *Christ Is All*; *Believers*.

drives me to publish this present work is because it sheds significant light on this vital matter.

***All this plays heavily into the doctrine of justification by faith.*** Christ fulfilled the law of God given to Israel through Moses. And it is this obedience which is the righteousness that is imputed to the sinner the moment he trusts Christ and is thus united to him. For my supporting arguments, see my *Christ's Obedience Imputed*. I now argue that it is by taking a proper, scriptural view of the promises of the old covenant that we get an excellent insight into the nature of 'righteousness'. This, of course, is of the utmost importance. It plays very significantly into imputed righteousness; that is to say, justification through faith in Christ alone, on the basis of God's free grace alone. The old-covenant promises of reward through meeting the required conditions show us yet again that righteousness is not just pardon but that it is positive, practical obedience to the commandments of God under his law. This is utterly basic to the new-covenant doctrine of imputed righteousness. Israel, under the Mosaic covenant, had to obey God's commandments. Reward followed, but the promises were conditional. This principle is written large across the old covenant: 'If... then...'. 'Do... and live' (Lev. 18:5; Rom. 9:33 – 10:5; Gal. 3:10-12). Christ obeyed his Father under the law. These are more than facts; they undergird justification by faith in the new covenant. This vital point merits setting out in a little more detail.

Just before I do, let me very briefly indicate the biblical justification for calling upon the old covenant in this important matter. In fact, I should put it more strongly than that. We will not understand the new covenant in this area unless we take full account of the old.

Take sanctification (both positional and progressive).[35] This cannot be divorced from justification. Notice how Peter (actually, God through Peter) uses the old covenant to enforce the new on progressive sanctification: 'As he who called you is holy, you also be holy in all your conduct,

---

[35] See my *Fivefold*; *Positional*.

because it is written: "Be holy, for I am holy'" (1 Pet. 1:15-16). Where was it 'written'? In the old covenant, of course, and not once but three times (Lev. 11:44-45; 19:2; 20:7). But Peter repeats it to believers in the new covenant. Nothing could be clearer. Whichever covenant, old or new, second best will not do for God. This undergirded the old covenant: temple, priest, sacrifice and people must be holy. The same applies in the new.[36] Indeed, if God set such a high standard for Israel under the old covenant, how high the standard must be for believers under the new! We know there is a glorious 'much more' about the new covenant.[37] So it is with the believer's holiness.

Similarly, all this pertains to 'righteousness'. Look how Paul argues 'righteousness' based on principles which long pre-dated the new covenant. In the most important case, it even pre-dated the old covenant:

> What then shall we say was gained by Abraham, our forefather according to the flesh? For if Abraham was justified by works, he has something to boast about, but not before God. For what does the Scripture say? 'Abraham believed God, and it was counted to him as righteousness'. Now to the one who works, his wages are not counted as a gift but as his due. And to the one who does not work but believes in him who justifies the ungodly, his faith is counted as righteousness, just as David also speaks of the blessing of the one to whom God counts righteousness apart from works: 'Blessed are those whose lawless deeds are forgiven, and whose sins are covered; blessed is the man against whom the Lord will not count his sin'... For the promise to Abraham and his offspring that he would be heir of the world did not come through the law but through the righteousness of faith (Rom. 4:1-8,13).

Let me break in at this point. Paul is not arguing that the law plays no part in righteousness, and, consequently, no part in justification. Rather, he is making the point that no sinner

---

[36] See my *The Priesthood*.
[37] Put 'much more' and its equivalent into a Bible search engine! Try Rom. 5 for a start.

can be justified by the law, because no sinner can earn the requisite righteousness which can be obtained only by perfect obedience to the law. To let Paul continue:

> For the promise to Abraham and his offspring that he would be heir of the world did not come through the law but through the righteousness of faith. For if it is the adherents of the law who are to be the heirs, faith is null and the promise is void. For the law brings wrath, but where there is no law there is no transgression.
> That is why it depends on faith, in order that the promise may rest on grace and be guaranteed to all his offspring – not only to the adherent of the law but also to the one who shares the faith of Abraham, who is the father of us all, as it is written: 'I have made you the father of many nations' – in the presence of the God in whom he believed, who gives life to the dead and calls into existence the things that do not exist. In hope he believed against hope, that he should become the father of many nations, as he had been told: 'So shall your offspring be'. He did not weaken in faith when he considered his own body, which was as good as dead (since he was about a hundred years old), or when he considered the barrenness of Sarah's womb. No unbelief made him waver concerning the promise of God, but he grew strong in his faith as he gave glory to God, fully convinced that God was able to do what he had promised. That is why his faith was 'counted to him as righteousness'. But the words 'it was counted to him' were not written for his sake alone, but for ours also. It will be counted to us who believe in him who raised from the dead Jesus our Lord, who was delivered up for our trespasses and raised for our justification (Rom. 4:13-25).

Again:

> Abraham 'believed God, and it was counted to him as righteousness'... Know then that it is those of faith who are the sons of Abraham. And the Scripture, foreseeing that God would justify the Gentiles by faith, preached the gospel beforehand to Abraham, saying: 'In you shall all the nations be blessed'. So then, those who are of faith are blessed along with Abraham, the man of faith. For all who rely on works of the law are under a curse; for it is written: 'Cursed be everyone who does not abide by all things

written in the book of the law, and do them'. Now it is evident that no one is justified before God by the law, for 'The righteous shall live by faith'. But the law is not of faith, rather 'The one who does them shall live by them'. Christ redeemed us from the curse of the law by becoming a curse for us – for it is written: 'Cursed is everyone who is hanged on a tree' –so that in Christ Jesus the blessing of Abraham might come to the Gentiles, so that we might receive the promised Spirit through faith (Gal. 3:6-14).

It is conclusive. We will get no real comprehension of new-covenant righteousness unless we take full account of the principles of righteousness established by God in the days of the old covenant and before; namely, that righteousness involves works, obedience to law. With that in mind, let me take up the thread once again.

We know that Christ came into the world expressly to do his Father's will (Heb. 10:5-10), and that included obedience to the will of God expressed in the Mosaic law. Christ, therefore, became a man, a Jew, being born under the law (Gal. 4:4). Moreover, Christ, in his life, was fully obedient to the commands of the law, starting from his earliest days (Luke 2:27,39,41-42,49), through his life (Matt. 8:4; 17:24-27; Luke 17:14; and so on) and, in his death, suffered its penalty, curse and condemnation. Thus throughout his entire life and death he was always obedient to his Father, always pleasing him. As he himself said: 'I do nothing on my own authority, but speak just as the Father taught me... I always do the things that are pleasing to him' (John 8:28-29). Always! Not just in his dying on the cross! Of course, it all culminated on the cross, but Christ's entire life of obedience plays a vital part in the believer's justification. 'I lay down my life that I may take it up again. No one takes it from me, but I lay it down of my own accord. I have authority to lay it down, and I have authority to take it up again. This charge I have received from my Father' (John 10:17-18). 'I have not spoken on my own authority, but the Father who sent me has himself given me a commandment – what to say and what to speak... What I say, therefore, I say as the Father has told me' (John 12:49-50). 'I do as the Father has commanded me'

(John 14:31). In this way, both actively and passively, Christ established that righteousness which would justify the elect. 'It is accomplished', he was able to cry in triumph (John 19:30). God the Father demonstrated his total satisfaction – pleasure – in, by and with this completed work of his Son, and his full acceptance of it, by raising him from the dead, receiving him back in exaltation into glory, crowned in triumph (Ps. 24:7-10; Isa. 52:13; 53:12; Phil. 2:9-11; 1 Tim. 3:16). And this played into justification by faith. As the apostle asserted:

> [Christ] was delivered up for our trespasses and raised for our justification (Rom. 4:25).

In particular, for my present purpose, it is Christ's life of obedience under the law in connection with the old-covenant promises which is of concern:

> Although he [that is, Christ] was a son, he learned obedience through what he suffered. And being made perfect, he became the source of eternal salvation to all who obey him (Heb. 5:8-9).

Obedience under the law, of course. And we know what the law demanded; we have the scriptural mantra regarding the law: 'Do and live; fail to do and die':

> You shall follow my rules and keep my statutes and walk in them. I am the LORD your God. You shall therefore keep my statutes and my rules; if a person does them, he shall live by them: I am the LORD (Lev. 18:4-5).

> And behold, a lawyer stood up to put [Jesus] to the test, saying: 'Teacher, what shall I do to inherit eternal life?' He said to him: 'What is written in the law? How do you read it?' And he answered: 'You shall love the Lord your God with all your heart and with all your soul and with all your strength and with all your mind, and your neighbour as yourself'. And he said to him: 'You have answered correctly; do this, and you will live' (Luke 10:25-28).

> When [a man] has done what is just and right, and has been careful to observe all my statutes, he shall surely live. The soul who sins shall die... If a wicked person turns away

from all his sins that he has committed and keeps all my statutes and does what is just and right, he shall surely live; he shall not die. None of the transgressions that he has committed shall be remembered against him; for the righteousness that he has done he shall live (Ezek. 18:19-22).

[God] will render to each one according to his works: to those who by patience in well-doing seek for glory and honour and immortality, he will give eternal life; but for those who are self-seeking and do not obey the truth, but obey unrighteousness, there will be wrath and fury. There will be tribulation and distress for every human being who does evil, the Jew first and also the Greek, but glory and honour and peace for everyone who does good, the Jew first and also the Greek. For God shows no partiality... It is not the hearers of the law who are righteous before God, but the doers of the law who will be justified (Rom. 2:6-11,13).

Moses writes about the righteousness that is based on the law, that the person who does the commandments shall live by them (Rom. 10:5).

All who rely on works of the law are under a curse; for it is written: 'Cursed be everyone who does not abide by all things written in the book of the law, and do them'. Now it is evident that no one is justified before God by the law, for: 'The righteous shall live by faith'. But the law is not of faith, rather: 'The one who does them shall live by them' (Gal. 3:10-12).

It is precisely at this point that Christ's declared manifesto – which he issued at the start of his earthly ministry – plays such a significant role:

Do not think that I have come to abolish the law or the prophets; I have not come to abolish them but to fulfil them. For truly, I say to you, until heaven and earth pass away, not an iota, not a dot, will pass from the law until all is accomplished. Therefore whoever relaxes one of the least of these commandments and teaches others to do the same will be called least in the kingdom of heaven, but whoever does them and teaches them will be called great in the kingdom of heaven. For I tell you, unless your

79

righteousness exceeds that of the scribes and Pharisees, you will never enter the kingdom of heaven (Matt. 5:17-20).

No wonder, then, that Paul could be so categorical:

There is therefore now no condemnation for those who are in Christ Jesus. For the law of the Spirit of life has set you free in Christ Jesus from the law of sin and death. For God has done what the law, weakened by the flesh, could not do. By sending his own Son in the likeness of sinful flesh and for sin, he condemned sin in the flesh, in order that the righteous requirement of the law might be fulfilled in us, who walk not according to the flesh but according to the Spirit (Rom. 8:1-4).

For Christ is the end of the law for righteousness to everyone who believes (Rom. 10:4).

There are, it goes without saying, a great many other scriptures that feed into this, but I leave it there.

Jesus is unique in that he is the only man that has ever lived in order to fulfil the will of God, and that 'will' surely included the keeping and fulfilling of the law. Christ came into the world in order to fulfil it, as he said, and as the writer to the Hebrews took such pains to stress (Heb. 10:5-9), and he is the only man ever to come with that purpose, and carry it out. Since we ourselves can never produce any better righteousness that that of the Pharisees (if that!), the only way that our righteousness can exceed theirs is if the righteousness of Jesus is imputed to us. And it is vital to note that Matthew 5:17-20 speaks of far more than *suffering*, even unto *death*, under the law. Indeed, there is no suggestion whatsoever here of any connection between the Pharisees and death. It is all a question of *obedience* in *life*. Clearly, Christ was talking of positive obedience to the law.

So, with the old-covenant principle in mind:

The LORD rewards every man for his righteousness and his faithfulness (1 Sam. 26:23).

In light of that, reconsider the following passages from the Messianic point of view. In what follows I can distinctly hear Christ, addressing his Father, speaking in the words of the psalmist. He knew that:

> ...the rules [just decrees] of the LORD are true, and righteous altogether. More to be desired are they than gold, even much fine gold; sweeter also than honey and drippings of the honeycomb. Moreover, by them is your servant warned; in keeping them there is great reward (Ps. 19:9-11).

> [God] will render to a man according to his work (Ps. 62:12).

And here, I am convinced, is the sound of Christ's voice as he lays his righteous works under the law before his Father:

> Judge me, O LORD, according to my righteousness and according to the integrity that is in me (Ps. 7:8).

And here Christ acknowledges that his Father has heard and rewarded him for his faultless obedience under the law, his perfect righteousness:

> The LORD dealt with me according to my righteousness; according to the cleanness of my hands he rewarded me. For I have kept the ways of the LORD, and have not wickedly departed from my God. For all his rules [just decrees] were before me, and his statutes I did not put away from me. I was blameless before him, and I kept myself from my guilt. So the LORD has rewarded me according to my righteousness, according to the cleanness of my hands in his sight (Ps. 18:20-24).

And in these passages I can hear God the Father speaking to his Son (or of him):

> You are my Son; today I have begotten you. Ask of me, and I will make the nations your heritage, and the ends of the earth your possession. You shall break them with a rod of iron and dash them in pieces like a potter's vessel (Ps. 2:7-9).

> Behold, my servant shall act wisely; he shall be high and lifted up, and shall be exalted. As many were astonished at you – his appearance was so marred, beyond human semblance, and his form beyond that of the children of

mankind – so shall he sprinkle many nations. Kings shall shut their mouths because of him, for that which has not been told them they see, and that which they have not heard they understand (Isa. 52:13-15).

Yet it was the will of the LORD to crush him; he has put him to grief; when his soul makes an offering for guilt, he shall see his offspring; he shall prolong his days; the will of the LORD shall prosper in his hand. Out of the anguish of his soul he shall see and be satisfied; by his knowledge shall the righteous one, my servant, make many to be accounted righteous, and he shall bear their iniquities. Therefore I will divide him a portion with the many, and he shall divide the spoil with the strong, because he poured out his soul to death and was numbered with the transgressors; yet he bore the sin of many, and makes intercession for the transgressors (Isa. 53:10-12).

Christ Jesus, who, though he was in the form of God, did not count equality with God a thing to be grasped, but emptied himself, by taking the form of a servant, being born in the likeness of men. And being found in human form, he humbled himself by becoming obedient to the point of death, even death on a cross. Therefore God has highly exalted him and bestowed on him the name that is above every name, so that at the name of Jesus every knee should bow, in heaven and on earth and under the earth, and every tongue confess that Jesus Christ is Lord, to the glory of God the Father (Phil. 2:5-11).

This is how we must view the old-covenant promises. This is the point. It is not that we claim them in the spirit of the prosperity gospellers, but rather that we see how Christ, under the law, fulfilling the law, brought in everlasting righteousness for his elect. In earning the reward, he did not earn a righteousness for himself, of course, but merited a perfect righteousness for his people, a righteousness to be imputed to his elect as they come to faith and are united to the Redeemer. Believers can say of God:

For our sake he [that is, the Father] made him [that is, the Son] who knew no sin to be sin, so that in him we might become the righteousness of God (2 Cor. 5:21).

And for the sake of the elect, Christ pleaded his righteousness before his father. Supremely, the voice of Christ, addressing his Father on this ground, can be heard in his great high-priestly prayer:

> Father, the hour has come; glorify your Son that the Son may glorify you, since you have given him authority over all flesh, to give eternal life to all whom you have given him. And this is eternal life, that they know you, the only true God, and Jesus Christ whom you have sent. I glorified you on earth, having accomplished the work that you gave me to do. And now, Father, glorify me in your own presence with the glory that I had with you before the world existed.
> I have manifested your name to the people whom you gave me out of the world. Yours they were, and you gave them to me, and they have kept your word. Now they know that everything that you have given me is from you. For I have given them the words that you gave me, and they have received them and have come to know in truth that I came from you; and they have believed that you sent me. I am praying for them. I am not praying for the world but for those whom you have given me, for they are yours. All mine are yours, and yours are mine, and I am glorified in them. And I am no longer in the world, but they are in the world, and I am coming to you. Holy Father, keep them in your name, which you have given me, that they may be one, even as we are one. While I was with them, I kept them in your name, which you have given me. I have guarded them, and not one of them has been lost except the son of destruction, that the Scripture might be fulfilled. But now I am coming to you, and these things I speak in the world, that they may have my joy fulfilled in themselves. I have given them your word, and the world has hated them because they are not of the world, just as I am not of the world. I do not ask that you take them out of the world, but that you keep them from the evil one. They are not of the world, just as I am not of the world. Sanctify them in the truth; your word is truth. As you sent me into the world, so I have sent them into the world. And for their sake I consecrate myself, that they also may be sanctified in truth.
> I do not ask for these only, but also for those who will believe in me through their word, that they may all be one,

just as you, Father, are in me, and I in you, that they also
may be in us, so that the world may believe that you have
sent me. The glory that you have given me I have given to
them, that they may be one even as we are one, I in them
and you in me, that they may become perfectly one, so that
the world may know that you sent me and loved them even
as you loved me. Father, I desire that they also, whom you
have given me, may be with me where I am, to see my
glory that you have given me because you loved me before
the foundation of the world. O righteous Father, even
though the world does not know you, I know you, and these
know that you have sent me. I made known to them your
name, and I will continue to make it known, that the love
with which you have loved me may be in them, and I in
them (John 17:1-26).

And this is why we must not stop at the negative when
dealing with the promises of the old covenant. Thus,
justification by faith by the imputation of Christ's
righteousness in obedience is a glorious truth of the new
covenant. That which the law could not do, that which we
could not do, God through Christ has done. And it is all ours!
Let us trumpet it abroad!

***The cumulative effect of what has gone before shows that
we, as new-covenant theologians, rebut the ridiculous, but
often made, charge of antinomianism.*** We take it back to
where it rightly belongs. We don't divide the law of Moses
into bits, rejecting selected parts according to the dictates of
theologians and their systems of theology. The law is not a
menu for us to select from. We don't pick and mix. We take
all the law, use all the law, apply all the law, to our lives as
believers. And this includes both its conditions and its
promises. We have a more penetrating view of the law of
Christ than those who glibly dismiss us as antinomians. We
have a biblical view. We do not have a squeezed, cramped
view of the law, deduced from a theological template drawn
up in the 16th and 17th centuries, drawn up by men who had
a legal agenda, who produced documents based on the
teachings of the medieval Church, coloured by the
philosophical and tortuous inventions of the covenant

theologians of the 16th century. The law of Christ, we argue, is fixed in Scripture, in Scripture alone, not in Scripture filtered by the 1647 Westminster Confession or 1689 Particular Baptist Confession, or whatever. And we are duty bound to obey Christ's law. This is an absolute essential.

And this takes us to the next point.

***The positives of the new covenant.*** A proper consideration of the old-covenant promises highlights one of the great practical effects of the new covenant in the life of the believer. Whereas the old-covenant promises in question talked in material terms, the promises of the new covenant speak of spiritual – even eternal – benefits.

In other words, the spirit – the ethos – of the new covenant is very different to that of the old covenant. Believers are not primarily looking for material comfort, deliverance from every illness, difficulty or trouble. Oh, such things are very pleasant and eagerly desired and prayed for at times, I agree, but the believer's attitude is far removed from that of the prosperity-gospel devotee. Listen to the apostolic view of life, the difficult aspects of life, in particular:

> God is able to make all grace abound to you, so that having all sufficiency in all things at all times, you may abound in every good work (2 Cor. 9:8).

> Rejoice in the Lord always; again I will say, rejoice. Let your reasonableness be known to everyone. The Lord is at hand; do not be anxious about anything, but in everything by prayer and supplication with thanksgiving let your requests be made known to God. And the peace of God, which surpasses all understanding, will guard your hearts and your minds in Christ Jesus... I have learned in whatever situation I am to be content. I know how to be brought low, and I know how to abound. In any and every circumstance, I have learned the secret of facing plenty and hunger, abundance and need. I can do all things through him who strengthens me (Phil. 4:4-7,11-13).

> People who are depraved in mind and deprived of the truth, [imagine] that godliness is a means of gain. But godliness

with contentment is great gain, for we brought nothing into the world, and we cannot take anything out of the world. But if we have food and clothing, with these we will be content. But those who desire to be rich fall into temptation, into a snare, into many senseless and harmful desires that plunge people into ruin and destruction. For the love of money is a root of all kinds of evils. It is through this craving that some have wandered away from the faith and pierced themselves with many pangs (1 Tim. 6:5-10).

Recall the former days when, after you were enlightened, you endured a hard struggle with sufferings, sometimes being publicly exposed to reproach and affliction, and sometimes being partners with those so treated. For you had compassion on those in prison, and you joyfully accepted the plundering of your property, since you knew that you yourselves had a better possession and an abiding one. Therefore do not throw away your confidence, which has a great reward. For you have need of endurance, so that when you have done the will of God you may receive what is promised. For: 'Yet a little while, and the coming one will come and will not delay; but my righteous one shall live by faith, and if he shrinks back, my soul has no pleasure in him'. But we are not of those who shrink back and are destroyed, but of those who have faith and preserve their souls (Heb. 10:32-39).

Keep your life free from love of money, and be content with what you have, for he has said: 'I will never leave you nor forsake you' (Heb. 13:5).

The prosperity gospel, with its encouragement of believers to pray for and expect the best of material things – what James calls 'pleasures' – gets very close to falling foul of his statement:

You ask and do not receive, because you ask amiss, that you may spend it on your pleasures (Jas. 4:3).

What is making a mint of money, being offered a better job, the removal of backache, and the like, compared with knowing Christ and all he has accomplished, and knowing and enjoying him for ever? As Christ asked rhetorically:

What does it profit a man if he gains the whole world and loses (or forfeits) himself? (Luke 9:25).

This is why we must not stop at the negative when dealing with the promises of the old covenant.

***Confession of sin is still vital in the new covenant.*** The old-covenant promises demanded confession of sin. So does the new covenant:

> If we say we have no sin, we deceive ourselves, and the truth is not in us. If we confess our sins, he is faithful and just to forgive us our sins and to cleanse us from all unrighteousness. If we say we have not sinned, we make him a liar, and his word is not in us (1 John 8-10).

Here is an often neglected point: this passage, though it has relevance to unbelievers, was written to believers. We, as believers, confess our sin. It is a new-covenant duty or condition. Consider this:

> Confess your sins to one another and pray for one another, that you may be healed (Jas. 5:16).[38]

Note that this is mutual confession, a mutual acknowledgement of faults and offences, and is connected with healing. The 'mutual' it speaks of is believer-to-believer confession, not believer to elder. I see this linked to passages such as Matthew 18:15-35; 1 Corinthians 5:1-13; 11:29-31.

Of course, new-covenant confession of sin has nothing in common with papistical nonsense. Nor is it done in order to earn salvation. In Ephesus, new converts showed the way: 'Many of those who were now believers came, confessing and divulging their practices' (Acts 19:18). And their confession was not confined to lip; they acted in tandem with their word:

> And a number of those who had practiced magic arts brought their books together and burned them in the sight of all. And they counted the value of them and found it

---

[38] I will return to this in the following chapter.

came to fifty thousand pieces of silver. So the word of the Lord continued to increase and prevail mightily (Acts 19:19-20).

The old covenant made this principle of confession clear in its promises. The principle of confession comes over into the new covenant. And this is why we must not stop at the negative when dealing with the promises of the old covenant.

*Warnings leading to curses are part of the new covenant, whether stated or implied.* This is so little stressed today and yet the New Testament heavily underlines it in passage after passage. And the judgment is always declared to be of words and especially works:

Out of the abundance of the heart the mouth speaks. The good person out of his good treasure brings forth good, and the evil person out of his evil treasure brings forth evil. I tell you, on the day of judgment people will give account for every careless word they speak, for by your words you will be justified, and by your words you will be condemned (Matt. 12:34-37).

First, the absolute seriousness of what is being talked about:

Do not fear those who kill the body but cannot kill the soul. Rather fear him who can destroy both soul and body in hell (Matt. 10:28).

The initial aspect – faith in Christ. Or the lack of it, the refusal to believe:

Whoever does not believe [in Christ] is condemned already, because he has not believed in the name of the only Son of God... Whoever does not obey the Son shall not see life, but the wrath of God remains on him (John 3:18,36).

And so to passages which spell out the curses of the new covenant:

When the Son of Man comes in his glory, and all the angels with him, then he will sit on his glorious throne. Before him will be gathered all the nations, and he will separate people one from another as a shepherd separates the sheep from the goats. And he will place the sheep on his right, but the goats on the left. Then the King will say to those on his right: 'Come, you who are blessed by my Father, inherit the kingdom prepared for you from the foundation of the world. For I was hungry and you gave me food, I was thirsty and you gave me drink, I was a stranger and you welcomed me, I was naked and you clothed me, I was sick and you visited me, I was in prison and you came to me'. Then the righteous will answer him, saying: 'Lord, when did we see you hungry and feed you, or thirsty and give you drink? And when did we see you a stranger and welcome you, or naked and clothe you? And when did we see you sick or in prison and visit you?' And the King will answer them: 'Truly, I say to you, as you did it to one of the least of these my brothers, you did it to me'.

Then he will say to those on his left: 'Depart from me, you cursed, into the eternal fire prepared for the devil and his angels. For I was hungry and you gave me no food, I was thirsty and you gave me no drink, I was a stranger and you did not welcome me, naked and you did not clothe me, sick and in prison and you did not visit me'. Then they also will answer, saying: 'Lord, when did we see you hungry or thirsty or a stranger or naked or sick or in prison, and did not minister to you?' Then he will answer them, saying: 'Truly, I say to you, as you did not do it to one of the least of these, you did not do it to me'. And these will go away into eternal punishment, but the righteous into eternal life (Matt. 25:31-46).

I am the true vine, and my Father is the vinedresser. Every branch in me that does not bear fruit he takes away, and every branch that does bear fruit he prunes, that it may bear more fruit. Already you are clean because of the word that I have spoken to you. Abide in me, and I in you. As the branch cannot bear fruit by itself, unless it abides in the vine, neither can you, unless you abide in me. I am the vine; you are the branches. Whoever abides in me and I in him, he it is that bears much fruit, for apart from me you can do nothing. If anyone does not abide in me he is thrown away like a branch and withers; and the branches are gathered, thrown into the fire, and burned. If you abide in me, and my words abide in you, ask whatever you wish, and it will be done for you. By this my Father is glorified, that you bear much fruit and so prove to be my disciples. As the Father has loved me, so have I loved you. Abide in my love. If you keep my commandments, you will abide in my love, just as I have kept my Father's commandments and abide in his love. These things I have spoken to you, that my joy may be in you, and that your joy may be full. This is my commandment, that you love one another as I have loved you (John 15:1-12).

If our unrighteousness serves to show the righteousness of God, what shall we say? That God is unrighteous to inflict wrath on us? (I speak in a human way.) By no means! For then how could God judge the world? But if through my lie God's truth abounds to his glory, why am I still being condemned as a sinner? And why not do evil that good may come? – as some people slanderously charge us with saying. Their condemnation is just (Rom. 3:5-8).

Do not become proud, but fear. For if God did not spare the natural branches, neither will he spare you. Note then the kindness and the severity of God: severity toward those who have fallen, but God's kindness to you, provided you continue in his kindness. Otherwise you too will be cut off (Rom. 11:20-22).

Beloved, never avenge yourselves, but leave it to the wrath of God, for it is written: 'Vengeance is mine; I will repay, says the Lord' (Rom. 12:19).

We will all stand before the judgment seat of God... Each of us will give an account of himself to God (Rom. 14:10,12).

Every athlete exercises self-control in all things. They do it to receive a perishable wreath, but we an imperishable. So I do not run aimlessly; I do not box as one beating the air. But I discipline my body and keep it under control, lest after preaching to others I myself should be disqualified (1 Cor. 9:25-27).

Now I would remind you, brothers, of the gospel I preached to you, which you received, in which you stand, and by which you are being saved, if you hold fast to the word I preached to you – unless you believed in vain (1 Cor. 15:1-2).

We must all appear before the judgment seat of Christ, so that each one may receive what is due for what he has done in the body, whether good or evil (2 Cor. 5:10).

And you, who once were alienated and hostile in mind, doing evil deeds, he has now reconciled in his body of flesh by his death, in order to present you holy and blameless and above reproach before him, if indeed you continue in the faith, stable and steadfast, not shifting from the hope of the gospel that you heard, which has been proclaimed in all creation under heaven, and of which I, Paul, became a minister (Col. 1:21-23).

The Jews... killed both the Lord Jesus and the prophets, and drove us out, and displease God and oppose all mankind by hindering us from speaking to the Gentiles that they might be saved – so as always to fill up the measure of their sins. But wrath has come upon them at last! (1 Thess. 2:14-16).

...when the Lord Jesus is revealed from heaven with his mighty angels in flaming fire, inflicting vengeance on those who do not know God and on those who do not obey the gospel of our Lord Jesus. They will suffer the punishment of eternal destruction, away from the presence of the Lord and from the glory of his might (2 Thess. 1:7-9).

... those who are perishing, because they refused to love the truth and so be saved. Therefore God sends them a strong delusion, so that they may believe what is false, in order that all may be condemned who did not believe the truth but had pleasure in unrighteousness (2 Thess. 2:10-12).

Therefore we must pay much closer attention to what we have heard, lest we drift away from it. For since the message declared by angels proved to be reliable, and every transgression or disobedience received a just retribution, how shall we escape if we neglect such a great salvation? (Heb. 2:1-3).

Take care, brothers, lest there be in any of you an evil, unbelieving heart, leading you to fall away from the living God. But exhort one another every day, as long as it is called "today", that none of you may be hardened by the deceitfulness of sin. For we have come to share in Christ, if indeed we hold our original confidence firm to the end. As it is said: 'Today, if you hear his voice, do not harden your hearts as in the rebellion'... Therefore, while the promise of entering his rest still stands, let us fear lest any of you should seem to have failed to reach it... Let us therefore strive to enter that rest, so that no one may fall by the same sort of disobedience (Heb. 3:12-15; 4:1,11).

It is impossible, in the case of those who have once been enlightened, who have tasted the heavenly gift, and have shared in the Holy Spirit, and have tasted the goodness of the word of God and the powers of the age to come, and then have fallen away, to restore them again to repentance, since they are crucifying once again the Son of God to their own harm and holding him up to contempt. For land that has drunk the rain that often falls on it, and produces a crop useful to those for whose sake it is cultivated, receives a blessing from God. But if it bears thorns and thistles, it is worthless and near to being cursed, and its end is to be burned (Heb. 6:4-8).[39]

If we go on sinning deliberately after receiving the knowledge of the truth, there no longer remains a sacrifice for sins, but a fearful expectation of judgment, and a fury of fire that will consume the adversaries. Anyone who has set aside the law of Moses dies without mercy on the evidence of two or three witnesses. How much worse punishment, do you think, will be deserved by the one who has trampled underfoot the Son of God, and has profaned the blood of the covenant by which he was sanctified, and has outraged the Spirit of grace? For we know him who said: 'Vengeance is mine; I will repay'. And again: 'The Lord will judge his people'. It is a fearful thing to fall into the hands of the living God (Heb. 10:26- 31).

Yet a little while, and the coming one will come and will not delay; but my righteous one shall live by faith, and if he shrinks back, my soul has no pleasure in him (Heb. 10:37-38).

---

[39] I admit, of course, that it goes on: 'Though we speak in this way, yet in your case, beloved, we feel sure of better things – things that belong to salvation. For God is not unjust so as to overlook your work and the love that you have shown for his name in serving the saints, as you still do. And we desire each one of you to show the same earnestness to have the full assurance of hope until the end, so that you may not be sluggish, but imitators of those who through faith and patience inherit the promises' (Heb. 6:9-12).

Therefore, since we are surrounded by so great a cloud of witnesses, let us also lay aside every weight, and the sin which clings so closely, and let us run with endurance the race that is set before us, looking to Jesus, the founder and perfecter of our faith, who for the joy that was set before him endured the cross, despising the shame, and is seated at the right hand of the throne of God. Consider him who endured from sinners such hostility against himself, so that you may not grow weary or fainthearted. In your struggle against sin you have not yet resisted to the point of shedding your blood. And have you forgotten the exhortation that addresses you as sons? 'My son, do not regard lightly the discipline of the Lord, nor be weary when reproved by him. For the Lord disciplines the one he loves, and chastises every son whom he receives'. It is for discipline that you have to endure. God is treating you as sons. For what son is there whom his father does not discipline? If you are left without discipline, in which all have participated, then you are illegitimate children and not sons. Besides this, we have had earthly fathers who disciplined us and we respected them. Shall we not much more be subject to the Father of spirits and live? For they disciplined us for a short time as it seemed best to them, but he disciplines us for our good, that we may share his holiness. For the moment all discipline seems painful rather than pleasant, but later it yields the peaceful fruit of righteousness to those who have been trained by it. Therefore lift your drooping hands and strengthen your weak knees, and make straight paths for your feet, so that what is lame may not be put out of joint but rather be healed. Strive for peace with everyone, and for the holiness without which no one will see the Lord. See to it that no one fails to obtain the grace of God; that no 'root of bitterness' springs up and causes trouble, and by it many become defiled; that no one is sexually immoral or unholy like Esau, who sold his birthright for a single meal. For you know that afterward, when he desired to inherit the blessing, he was rejected, for he found no chance to repent, though he sought it with tears... See that you do not refuse him who is speaking. For if they did not escape when they refused him who warned them on earth, much less will we escape if we reject him who warns from heaven (Heb. 12:1-17,25).

If anyone suffers as a Christian, let him not be ashamed, but let him glorify God in that name. For it is time for judgment to begin at the household of God; and if it begins with us, what will be the outcome for those who do not obey the gospel of God? (1 Pet. 4:16-17).

I do not apologise for such extended extracts. I really want to set out the very strong emphasis the New Testament gives to this aspect of the new covenant. I do so because it is so little stressed today. Why?

Finally, just as the curses of the new covenant are far greater than those of the old covenant, so, too, are its final and eternal blessings. Here is just the merest sample of the relevant passages of Scripture, some of which could be placed in the previous section also.

***The eternal blessings of the new covenant.*** This is what I am referring to:

Blessed are those who are persecuted for righteousness' sake, for theirs is the kingdom of heaven. Blessed are you when others revile you and persecute you and utter all kinds of evil against you falsely on my account. Rejoice and be glad, for your reward is great in heaven, for so they persecuted the prophets who were before you (Matt. 5:10-12).

When you give to the needy, sound no trumpet before you, as the hypocrites do in the synagogues and in the streets, that they may be praised by others. Truly, I say to you, they have received their reward. But when you give to the needy, do not let your left hand know what your right hand is doing, so that your giving may be in secret. And your Father who sees in secret will reward you... When you pray, you must not be like the hypocrites. For they love to stand and pray in the synagogues and at the street corners, that they may be seen by others. Truly, I say to you, they have received their reward. But when you pray, go into your room and shut the door and pray to your Father who is in secret. And your Father who sees in secret will reward you... When you fast, anoint your head and wash your face, that your fasting may not be seen by others but by your

Father who is in secret. And your Father who sees in secret will reward you (Matt. 6:2-6,17-18).[40]

The one who receives a prophet because he is a prophet will receive a prophet's reward, and the one who receives a righteous person because he is a righteous person will receive a righteous person's reward. And whoever gives one of these little ones even a cup of cold water because he is a disciple, truly, I say to you, he will by no means lose his reward (Matt. 10:41-42).

If anyone would come after me, let him deny himself and take up his cross and follow me. For whoever would save his life will lose it, but whoever loses his life for my sake will find it. For what will it profit a man if he gains the whole world and forfeits his soul? Or what shall a man give in return for his soul? For the Son of Man is going to come with his angels in the glory of his Father, and then he will repay each person according to what he has done (Matt. 16:24-27).

No one can lay a foundation other than that which is laid, which is Jesus Christ. Now if anyone builds on the foundation with gold, silver, precious stones, wood, hay, straw – each one's work will become manifest, for the Day will disclose it, because it will be revealed by fire, and the fire will test what sort of work each one has done. If the work that anyone has built on the foundation survives, he will receive a reward. If anyone's work is burned up, he will suffer loss, though he himself will be saved, but only as through fire (1 Cor. 3:11-15).

What then is my reward? That in my preaching I may present the gospel free of charge, so as not to make full use of my right in the gospel (1 Cor. 9:18).

Do you not know that in a race all the runners run, but only one receives the prize? So run that you may obtain it. Every athlete exercises self-control in all things. They do it to receive a perishable wreath, but we an imperishable (1 Cor. 9:24-25).

---

[40] In the following chapter I will address Matt. 6:25-34; 7:7-11.

My brothers, whom I love and long for, my joy and crown (Phil. 4:1).

Whatever you do, work heartily, as for the Lord and not for men, knowing that from the Lord you will receive the inheritance as your reward. You are serving the Lord Christ. For the wrongdoer will be paid back for the wrong he has done, and there is no partiality (Col. 3:23-25).

What is our hope or joy or crown of boasting before our Lord Jesus at his coming? Is it not you? For you are our glory and joy (1 Thess. 2:19-20).

I am already being poured out as a drink offering, and the time of my departure has come. I have fought the good fight, I have finished the race, I have kept the faith. Henceforth there is laid up for me the crown of righteousness, which the Lord, the righteous judge, will award to me on that day, and not only to me but also to all who have loved his appearing (2 Tim. 4:6-8).

Therefore do not throw away your confidence, which has a great reward. For you have need of endurance, so that when you have done the will of God you may receive what is promised (Heb. 10:35-36).

Blessed is the man who remains steadfast under trial, for when he has stood the test he will receive the crown of life, which God has promised to those who love him (Jas. 1:12).

Watch yourselves, so that you may not lose what we have worked for, but may win a full reward (2 John 1:8).

Do not fear what you are about to suffer. Behold, the devil is about to throw some of you into prison, that you may be tested, and for ten days you will have tribulation. Be faithful unto death, and I will give you the crown of life. He who has an ear, let him hear what the Spirit says to the churches. The one who conquers will not be hurt by the second death (Rev. 2:10-11).

I am coming soon. Hold fast what you have, so that no one may seize your crown. The one who conquers, I will make him a pillar in the temple of my God. Never shall he go out of it, and I will write on him the name of my God, and the name of the city of my God, the new Jerusalem, which comes down from my God out of heaven, and my own new name. He who has an ear, let him hear what the Spirit says to the churches (Rev. 3:11-13).

Your wrath came, and the time for the dead to be judged, and for rewarding your servants, the prophets and saints, and those who fear your name, both small and great, and for destroying the destroyers of the earth (Rev. 11:18).

I am coming soon, bringing my recompense with me, to repay each one for what he has done (Rev. 22:12).

Think of the indescribable joys in Christ – both now, and then, in the eternal state, forever! Isaac Watts sets out this truth so well in this hymn:

> *Curs'd be the man, for ever curs'd,*
> *That does one wilful sin commit;*
> *Death and damnation for the first,*
> *Without relief, and infinite.*
>
> *Thus Sinai roars, and round the earth*
> *Thunder, and fire, and vengeance flings;*
> *But Jesus, thy dear gasping breath*
> *And Calvary, say gentler things:*
>
> *'Pardon and grace, and boundless love,*
> *Streaming along a Saviour's blood;*
> *And life, and joy, and crowns above,*
> *Obtained by a dear bleeding God'.*
>
> *Hark! How he prays (the charming sound*
> *Dwells on his dying lips): 'Forgive!'*
> *And every groan and gaping wound*
> *Cries: 'Father, let the rebels live!'*
>
> *Go, ye that rest upon the law,*
> *And toil and seek salvation there,*
> *Look to the flame that Moses saw,*
> *And shrink, and tremble, and despair.*
>
> *But I'll retire beneath the cross;*
> *Saviour, at thy dear feet I'll lie!*
> *And the keen sword that justice draws,*
> *Flaming and red, shall pass me by.*

This is why we must not stop at the negative when dealing with the promises of the old covenant.

Let Peter bring us to the close of this chapter:

> Since all these things [that is, the present heavens and earth] are thus to be dissolved, what sort of people ought you to be in lives of holiness and godliness, waiting for and hastening the coming of the day of God, because of which the heavens will be set on fire and dissolved, and the heavenly bodies will melt as they burn! But according to his promise we are waiting for new heavens and a new earth in which righteousness dwells. Therefore, beloved, since you are waiting for these, be diligent to be found by him without spot or blemish, and at peace. And count the patience of our Lord as salvation, just as our beloved brother Paul also wrote to you according to the wisdom given him, as he does in all his letters when he speaks in them of these matters. There are some things in them that are hard to understand, which the ignorant and unstable twist to their own destruction, as they do the other Scriptures. You therefore, beloved, knowing this beforehand, take care that you are not carried away with the error of lawless people and lose your own stability. But grow in the grace and knowledge of our Lord and Saviour Jesus Christ. To him be the glory both now and to the day of eternity. Amen (2 Pet. 3:11-18).

Believers should not be taken up with things to be burned up at the last day. Rather, waiting for, looking for, their eternal glory in Christ, they should set their hearts and minds on Christ, not on things of the earth, and concentrate on their progressive sanctification, growing increasingly in likeness to their Saviour, the Lord Jesus Christ (Col. 3:1-11). This is what the theology of the new covenant teaches and emphasises!

# *Objections*

But what about the glorious assurance of the gospel?

*The glorious assurance of the gospel.* This is what I am referring to:

> We know that for those who love God all things work together for good, for those who are called according to his purpose (Rom. 8:28).

Or, as it may be rendered:

> We know that God causes all things to work together for good to those who love God, to those who are called according to his purpose.

'God causes all things to work together for good to those who love God'. Surely this teaches the prosperity gospel, does it not? According to the prosperity gospeller, it does. And that means that the believer is never ill, never meets any setback, never suffers, but always has the best of everything.

Hmm! Look at the context. I have already quoted it, but it requires repeating now. Grabbing texts out of context is fatal. Listen to Paul's reasoned argument, worked out over several verses:

> I consider that the sufferings of this present time are not worth comparing with the glory that is to be revealed to us. For the creation waits with eager longing for the revealing of the sons of God. For the creation was subjected to futility, not willingly, but because of him who subjected it, in hope that the creation itself will be set free from its bondage to corruption and obtain the freedom of the glory of the children of God. For we know that the whole creation has been groaning together in the pains of childbirth until now. And not only the creation, but we ourselves, who have the firstfruits of the Spirit, groan inwardly as we wait eagerly for adoption as sons, the redemption of our bodies. For in this hope we were saved. Now hope that is seen is not hope. For who hopes for what he sees? But if we hope

for what we do not see, we wait for it with patience (Rom. 8:18-25).

The apostle goes on:

> Likewise the Spirit helps us in our weakness. For we do not know what to pray for as we ought, but the Spirit himself intercedes for us with groanings too deep for words. And he who searches hearts knows what is the mind of the Spirit, because the Spirit intercedes for the saints according to the will of God. *And we know that for those who love God all things work together for good, for those who are called according to his purpose* (Rom. 8:26-28).

Comment is surely superfluous. In this fallen world, the believer suffers with the rest of creation; he is not exempt. But he has the assurance that in all his sufferings, as well as in all his joys, God is working everlasting good, spiritual good, to and for him. Look how the apostle drives home the point. In all the vicissitudes of life, in all the sufferings a believer meets because he is in Christ – *because* he is in Christ, I stress – he can rest assured that God is working eternal glory and eternal good, spiritual good, for him:

> For those whom he foreknew he also predestined to be conformed to the image of his Son, in order that he might be the firstborn among many brothers. And those whom he predestined he also called, and those whom he called he also justified, and those whom he justified he also glorified. What then shall we say to these things? If God is for us, who can be against us? He who did not spare his own Son but gave him up for us all, how will he not also with him graciously give us all things? Who shall bring any charge against God's elect? It is God who justifies. Who is to condemn? Christ Jesus is the one who died – more than that, who was raised – who is at the right hand of God, who indeed is interceding for us. Who shall separate us from the love of Christ? Shall tribulation, or distress, or persecution, or famine, or nakedness, or danger, or sword? As it is written: 'For your sake we are being killed all the day long; we are regarded as sheep to be slaughtered'. No, in all these things we are more than conquerors through him who loved us. For I am sure that neither death nor life, nor angels nor

rulers, nor things present nor things to come, nor powers, nor height nor depth, nor anything else in all creation, will be able to separate us from the love of God in Christ Jesus our Lord (Rom. 8:29-39).

As the apostle told the Corinthians:

We do not lose heart. Though our outer self is wasting away, our inner self is being renewed day by day. For this light momentary affliction is preparing for us an eternal weight of glory beyond all comparison, as we look not to the things that are seen but to the things that are unseen. For the things that are seen are transient, but the things that are unseen are eternal. For we know that if the tent that is our earthly home is destroyed, we have a building from God, a house not made with hands, eternal in the heavens. For in this tent we groan, longing to put on our heavenly dwelling, if indeed by putting it on we may not be found naked. For while we are still in this tent, we groan, being burdened – not that we would be unclothed, but that we would be further clothed, so that what is mortal may be swallowed up by life. He who has prepared us for this very thing is God, who has given us the Spirit as a guarantee (2 Cor. 4:16 – 5:5).

William Cowper (who by bitter experience had plumbed the depths of human sorrow) got it right when he wrote:

*God moves in a mysterious way*
*His wonders to perform;*
*He plants his footsteps in the sea,*
*And rides upon the storm.*

*Deep in unfathomable mines*
*Of never-failing skill,*
*He treasures up his bright designs,*
*And works his sov'reign will.*

*Ye fearful saints, fresh courage take,*
*The clouds ye so much dread*
*Are big with mercy, and shall break*
*In blessings on your head.*

*Judge not the Lord by feeble sense,*
*But trust him for his grace;*
*Behind a frowning providence*
*He hides a smiling face.*

*His purposes will ripen fast,*
*Unfolding ev'ry hour;*
*The bud may have a bitter taste,*
*But sweet will be the flower.*

*Blind unbelief is sure to err,*
*And scan his work in vain;*
*God is his own interpreter,*
*And he will make it plain.*

Romans 8:28 does not teach the prosperity gospel.

But what about the many cures wrought by Christ and the apostles? Aren't there scores of references which speak of such? Don't they talk of healing as an integral part of the new covenant? Doesn't this tell us that the prosperity gospel has got more to recommend it than I have allowed? And what about: 'By his [that is, Christ's] wounds we are healed' (Isa. 53:5)?

Well, Peter's quotation of the passage sets it in context:

He himself bore our sins in his body on the cross, so that we might die to sins and live for righteousness; by his wounds you have been healed (1 Pet. 2:24).

It all hinges on the 'healed', the use Peter makes of the word. He could have been speaking about healing from physical or mental disease, yes, but the context is concerned with sin, with no suggestion of illness.[41] And if Peter was thinking of illness, it leaves us with the problem of the scripturally-recorded cases of godly people who do suffer illness, sometime incurable illness, even over many pain-ridden years.

Nevertheless, I readily grant that physical cures were wrought by the Spirit through Christ and the apostles, Yes,

---

[41] C.H.Spurgeon, for one, had no doubt that the apostle was referring to sin. See Spurgeon sermons 1143 and 2887.

indeed. But those cures are biblically described as signs, wonders and miracles. And with good reason. For 'signs, wonders and miracles' are terms which carry a technical meaning, a specific meaning. The miracles wrought through Christ and the apostles vindicated their persons and their message. In addition, they illustrated – as a kind of living parable – the gospel they preached. Let me prove it.

***The miracles as signs.*** John the Baptist, languishing in prison, sent a message to Christ: 'When John heard in prison about the deeds of the Christ, he sent word by his disciples'. He asked the Lord a question. Now whether John was concerned for himself, or was asking for the sake of his followers, does not matter for my present purpose. There is no doubt about what he had in mind:

> Are you the one who is to come, or shall we look for another?

That was what was on John's mind. Was Jesus the Messiah, after all? Jesus replied:

> Go and tell John what you hear and see: the blind receive their sight and the lame walk, lepers are cleansed and the deaf hear, and the dead are raised up, and the poor have good news preached to them. And blessed is the one who is not offended by me (Matt. 11:2-6).

Notice that Christ did not give John a straight 'Yes'. Indeed, it might almost be said that his answer was oblique. So how did Christ's indirect answer meet John's need? Why didn't Jesus issue a simple 'Yes'? 'Yes' is what he meant. So why didn't he say it straight out? Jesus clearly had a larger end in view. John, of course, would have known what Jesus was getting at. And if his followers were still in the dark, John would have set them right. Christ was referring to Isaiah and his prophecy concerning Jesus himself, his coming as the Messiah, and the evidential testimony God would give him:

> Behold, your God will come with vengeance, with the recompense of God. He will come and save you. Then the eyes of the blind shall be opened, and the ears of the deaf

unstopped; then shall the lame man leap like a deer, and the tongue of the mute sing for joy (Isa. 35:4-6).

You see? The miracles which Christ wrought bore witness to his person and his message, justifying his claims, validating his assertions. Yes, those who were cured received the benefit of healing, but Christ's main purpose was not their cure but the Spirit's vindication of himself, a vindication of his message – the gospel – and an illustration of it.

I am not whistling in the dark. When Philip asked Christ to show them the Father, the Lord Jesus immediately replied:

Have I been with you so long, and you still do not know me, Philip? Whoever has seen me has seen the Father. How can you say: 'Show us the Father'? Do you not believe that I am in the Father and the Father is in me? The words that I say to you I do not speak on my own authority, but the Father who dwells in me does his works. Believe me that I am in the Father and the Father is in me, or else believe on account of the works themselves (John 14:9-11).

When Christ urged Philip to 'believe on account of the works', can there be any doubt but that he was referring to his miraculous signs? Moreover, within that same discourse, Christ broadened the scope; talking of unbelievers, specifically contemporary Jewish unbelievers, he declared:

If I had not done among them the works that no one else did, they would not be guilty of sin, but now they have seen and hated both me and my Father (John 15:24).

Once again, the signs vindicated Christ and his message. Those who rejected the signs were rejecting both him and his gospel. The signs, the person of Christ and the gospel were inseparable.

Right at the start of his ministry, as early as Mark 2, in a passage of the utmost significance in this regard, Christ had put this beyond all vestige of doubt:

And when he [that is, Christ] returned to Capernaum after some days, it was reported that he was at home. And many were gathered together, so that there was no more room, not even at the door. And he was preaching the word to them.

And they came, bringing to him a paralytic carried by four men. And when they could not get near him because of the crowd, they removed the roof above him, and when they had made an opening, they let down the bed on which the paralytic lay. And when Jesus saw their faith, he said to the paralytic: 'Son, your sins are forgiven'. Now some of the scribes were sitting there, questioning in their hearts, 'Why does this man speak like that? He is blaspheming! Who can forgive sins but God alone?' And immediately Jesus, perceiving in his spirit that they thus questioned within themselves, said to them: 'Why do you question these things in your hearts? Which is easier, to say to the paralytic: "Your sins are forgiven", or to say: "Rise, take up your bed and walk"? But that you may know that the Son of Man has authority on earth to forgive sins' – he said to the paralytic – 'I say to you, rise, pick up your bed, and go home'. And he rose and immediately picked up his bed and went out before them all, so that they were all amazed and glorified God, saying: 'We never saw anything like this!' (Mark 2:1-12).

Clearly, it was the forgiveness of the man's sins that was the important thing, not the physical cure. The cure of his paralysis, though of tremendous benefit to the paralytic, and a huge encouragement to his friends, served to confirm, to the watching, doubtful crowd, Christ's power and right to forgive sins. Above all, it showed that it was the forgiveness of sins which overrode the physical cure.[42] The miraculous cure, accompanied by Christ's explanation, set the tone for all the teaching signs which would convey this vital truth to the people.

The point is set out in the letter to the Hebrews:

How shall we escape if we neglect such a great salvation? It was declared at first by the Lord, and it was attested to us by those who heard, while God also bore witness by signs

---

[42] Even in his healing of Malchus' ear, Christ displayed his power and compassion (Luke 22:51; John 18:10).

and wonders and various miracles and by gifts of the Holy
Spirit distributed according to his will (Heb. 2:3-4).[43]

And we have the following from John:

> Jesus did many other signs in the presence of the disciples,
> which are not written in this book; but these are written so
> that you may believe that Jesus is the Christ, the Son of
> God, and that by believing you may have life in his name
> (John 20:30-31).

More than that, Christ was himself the sign. As Simeon,
addressing Mary, declared:

> Behold, this child [that is, Christ] is appointed for the fall
> and rising of many in Israel, and for a sign that is opposed
> (and a sword will pierce through your own soul also), so
> that thoughts from many hearts may be revealed (Luke
> 2:34-35).

When we come to the Acts of the Apostles, the evidence is
overwhelming. See Acts 2:22,43; 3:1-26; 4:8-16,29-31; 5:12;
6:8; 8:6-7,13; 10:36-43; 14:3; 15:12; 19:11-12; 20:7-12;
28:1-10.

Paul could declare:

> I will not venture to speak of anything except what Christ
> has accomplished through me to bring the Gentiles to
> obedience – by word and deed, by the power of signs and
> wonders, by the power of the Spirit of God – so that from
> Jerusalem and all the way around to Illyricum I have
> fulfilled the ministry of the gospel of Christ (Rom. 15:18-
> 19).

---

[43] Depending on the manuscripts, Christ had spoken of it at the end
of Mark: "'These signs will accompany those who believe: in my
name they will cast out demons; they will speak in new tongues;
they will pick up serpents with their hands; and if they drink any
deadly poison, it will not hurt them; they will lay their hands on the
sick, and they will recover". So then the Lord Jesus, after he had
spoken to them, was taken up into heaven and sat down at the right
hand of God. And they went out and preached everywhere, while
the Lord worked with them and confirmed the message by
accompanying signs' (Mark 16:17-20).

As he told the Corinthians:

> I was not at all inferior to these super-apostles, even though I am nothing. The signs of a true apostle were performed among you with utmost patience, with signs and wonders and mighty works (2 Cor. 12:11-12).

It is patent. The signs were marks granted by God to Christ and the apostles to vindicate them and their message.

Jesus, of course, knew the Jewish mind; he was well aware of their clamour for signs:

> Unless you see signs and wonders you will not believe (John 4:48).

Indeed, they stipulated such from him:

> What sign do you do, that we may see and believe you? What work do you perform? (John 6:30).

That was not the only occasion: 'Teacher, we wish to see a sign from you', they demanded. I use 'demanded' because, although their request seemed politeness itself, Christ could read their hearts. He let them know that he knew what they were thinking, doing so in no uncertain terms:

> An evil and adulterous generation seeks for a sign, but no sign will be given to it except the sign of the prophet Jonah. For just as Jonah was three days and three nights in the belly of the great fish, so will the Son of Man be three days and three nights in the heart of the earth. The men of Nineveh will rise up at the judgment with this generation and condemn it, for they repented at the preaching of Jonah, and behold, something greater than Jonah is here. The queen of the South will rise up at the judgment with this generation and condemn it, for she came from the ends of the earth to hear the wisdom of Solomon, and behold, a greater than Solomon is here (Matt. 12:38-42).

What is more, attesting miracles were not enough:

> Though he had done so many signs before them, they [that is, the Jews] still did not believe in him (John 12:37).

107

And this was as Isaiah had predicted (Isa. 6:1-13; 53:1; John 12:38-41). And when 'many even of the authorities believed in him':

> ...for fear of the Pharisees they did not confess it, so that they would not be put out of the synagogue; for they loved the glory that comes from man more than the glory that comes from God (John 12:42-43).

The distressing fact is that not even Christ's resurrection would convince the sceptical Jews, unwilling as they were to believe him:

> If they do not hear Moses and the prophets, neither will they be convinced if someone should rise from the dead (Luke 16:31).

But, for those who had a heart to see, Christ's resurrection and his subsequent appearances were – and remain – convincing:

> Jesus did many other signs in the presence of the disciples, which are not written in this book [that is, John's Gospel]; but these are written so that you may believe that Jesus is the Christ, the Son of God, and that by believing you may have life in his name (John 20:30-31; see John 20 and 21, for instance).

> [Christ] presented himself alive to them [that is, the apostles] after his suffering by many proofs, appearing to them during forty days and speaking about the kingdom of God (Acts 1:3).[44]

As for the body of Christ's miracles, occasionally it would appear that some Jews, perhaps many, were convinced by them:

> A large crowd was following him, because they saw the signs that he was doing on the sick... When the people saw the sign that he had done [the feeding of the five thousand],

---

[44] Put 'resurrection' and 'raised' into a Bible search-engine to see how frequently the early preachers spoke of Christ's resurrection, as recorded in Acts, for instance.

they said: 'This is indeed the Prophet who is to come into the world!' (John 6:2,14).

The sad truth is, however, even when they saw the signs, signs they had demanded, the Jews still would not really believe. Christ told them so:

> Truly, truly, I say to you, you are seeking me, not because you saw signs, but because you ate your fill of the loaves (John 6:26).

And the Lord Jesus immediately went on to make the point that, in any case, they should not be thinking about the material, but the spiritual; concentrating, not on the temporal, but the eternal:

> Do not work for the food that perishes, but for the food that endures to eternal life, which the Son of Man will give to you. For on him God the Father has set his seal (John 6:26-27).

You see, the prosperity gospellers are doing nothing but repeat the old mistake of the Jews, and getting their priorities wrong! In this way they fall foul of Christ's plain teaching.

As I say, the Jews, even when they saw the signs, still did not truly believe. They even ridiculously attributed Christ's power to Beelzebul:

> Then a demon-oppressed man who was blind and mute was brought to him, and he healed him, so that the man spoke and saw. And all the people were amazed, and said: 'Can this be the Son of David?' But when the Pharisees heard it, they said: 'It is only by Beelzebul, the prince of demons, that this man casts out demons' (Matt. 12:22-24).

Jesus promptly quashed that nonsense. 'Knowing their thoughts, he said to them':

> Every kingdom divided against itself is laid waste, and no city or house divided against itself will stand. And if Satan casts out Satan, he is divided against himself. How then will his kingdom stand? And if I cast out demons by Beelzebul, by whom do your sons cast them out? Therefore they will be your judges. But if it is by the Spirit of God

that I cast out demons, then the kingdom of God has come upon you. Or how can someone enter a strong man's house and plunder his goods, unless he first binds the strong man? Then indeed he may plunder his house. Whoever is not with me is against me, and whoever does not gather with me scatters (Matt. 12:25-30).

Take the blind man in John 9.[45] The disciples wanted to know who was responsible for the man's blindness – his parents or the man himself. Whose sin was it? Jesus told them plainly:

> It was not that this man sinned, or his parents, but that the works of God might be displayed in him (John 9:3).

'The works of God'. What works? The ability to make the physically blind to see, yes, but above all the power to give sight to the spiritually blind. In other words, the sign – the miraculous cure of the man's blindness – would vindicate Christ, would confirm that he was the long-expected Messiah. On being questioned, the man himself stated plainly that he got the message, that he saw the truth, that he now knew and was prepared to own who and what Jesus was. As he told the Jewish bigwigs:

> How can a man who is a sinner do such signs?... He is a prophet... We know that God does not listen to sinners, but if anyone is a worshipper of God and does his will, God listens to him. Never since the world began has it been heard that anyone opened the eyes of a man born blind. If this man were not from God, he could do nothing (John 9:16-17,31-33).

And so to the punch line. As Jesus explained:

> For judgment I came into this world, that those who do not see may see, and those who see may become blind (John 9:39).

It was not physical blindness, but spiritual blindness that Christ was concerned with above all.

---

[45] See also John 11:4,15,40,47; 12:10-11,18-19,37.

It is just the same today. And this is what the new covenant is about. The prosperity gospellers want us to repeat the fundamental mistake of the Fathers who, as we have seen, in so many vital areas went back to the old covenant. This, in essence, is what the prosperity gospellers are doing by concentrating on the physical. Jesus is concerned with, and wants us to be concerned with, the spiritual.

But what about these two passages from Matthew? Here is the first:

> Therefore I tell you, do not be anxious about your life, what you will eat or what you will drink, nor about your body, what you will put on. Is not life more than food, and the body more than clothing? Look at the birds of the air: they neither sow nor reap nor gather into barns, and yet your heavenly Father feeds them. Are you not of more value than they? And which of you by being anxious can add a single hour to his span of life? And why are you anxious about clothing? Consider the lilies of the field, how they grow: they neither toil nor spin, yet I tell you, even Solomon in all his glory was not arrayed like one of these. But if God so clothes the grass of the field, which today is alive and tomorrow is thrown into the oven, will he not much more clothe you, O you of little faith? Therefore do not be anxious, saying: 'What shall we eat?' or 'What shall we drink?' or 'What shall we wear?' For the Gentiles [that is, pagans, unbelievers] seek after all these things, and your heavenly Father knows that you need them all. But seek first the kingdom of God and his righteousness, and all these things will be added to you. Therefore do not be anxious about tomorrow, for tomorrow will be anxious for itself. Sufficient for the day is its own trouble (Matt. 6:25-34)?

And this is the second from Matthew:

> Ask, and it will be given to you; seek, and you will find; knock, and it will be opened to you. For everyone who asks receives, and the one who seeks finds, and to the one who knocks it will be opened. Or which one of you, if his son asks him for bread, will give him a stone? Or if he asks for

a fish, will give him a serpent? If you then, who are evil, know how to give good gifts to your children, how much more will your Father who is in heaven give good things to those who ask him! (Matt. 7:7-11)?

I said I would return to these passages. Surely they teach the prosperity gospel, don't they? Far from it! In fact, the prosperity gospel turns both passages on their head. Let me explain.

The tone of the Matthew 6 passage is an appeal or command to believers not to be anxious when faced with material, daily concerns – food, clothing and health, and so on. Yet these are the very things that the prosperity gospel majors on. Further, it stresses that believers will have the best of health, jobs, homes, clothes, food and all the rest of it. But Jesus says nothing of the sort. He does not forbid the believer's anxiety over material things on the ground of the provision of plenty. His emphasis is entirely on the spiritual. Christ commands his people to leave such concerns – yes, those just concerns – to their Father's care to deal with. Their priority must be the spiritual – 'the kingdom of God and his righteousness' – leaving God to give what he sees best for the believer in terms of health and wealth (or lack of it). And he will give believers a sufficiency. Of that they may be sure, and set their hearts at rest. This is the point. Nobody in his right mind could claim that Christ was teaching the prosperity gospel here. As Christ says, that has far more in common with pagans than believers!

And as for Matthew 7, the punch line in Luke's account of Christ's teaching sets it all in context:

> You then, who are evil, know how to give good gifts to your children, how much more will the heavenly Father give the Holy Spirit to those who ask him! (Luke 11:13).

The emphasis, yet again, is on the spiritual, not the material. But what about James 5? I am convinced that this passage belongs to the extraordinary apostolic era, just coming to its end, even as James was writing:

Is anyone among you suffering? Let him pray. Is anyone cheerful? Let him sing praise. Is anyone among you sick? Let him call for the elders of the church, and let them pray over him, anointing him with oil in the name of the Lord. And the prayer of faith will save the one who is sick, and the Lord will raise him up. And if he has committed sins, he will be forgiven. Therefore, confess your sins to one another and pray for one another, that you may be healed. The prayer of a righteous person has great power as it is working. Elijah was a man with a nature like ours, and he prayed fervently that it might not rain, and for three years and six months it did not rain on the earth. Then he prayed again, and heaven gave rain, and the earth bore its fruit (Jas. 5:13-18).

I am also convinced that something similar applies to 1 Corinthians 11, dealing, as it does, with the direct intervention of God in judgment by illness and death for the breakdown of church life at Corinth:

Anyone who eats and drinks [at the Lord's supper] without discerning the body eats and drinks judgment on himself. That is why many of you are weak and ill, and some have died. But if we judged ourselves truly, we would not be judged. But when we are judged by the Lord, we are disciplined so that we may not be condemned along with the world (1 Cor. 11:29-32).

In short, I do not see that these objections carry any weight against what I have set out. They certainly do not encourage us to adopt the prosperity gospel.

# Conclusion

This can be very short indeed. The prosperity gospel is wrong, and a source of great hurt to those who buy into it. This is not the way for believers to read and apply the promises of the old covenant. No! But those promises do speak today. They speak of Christ and the new covenant. So, while we rightly reject the teaching of the prosperity gospellers, let us set out the truth with boldness. As with everything else scriptural, all tends to the glory of Christ. For Christ is all (Col. 3:11), and in all things he must have the pre-eminence (Col. 1:15-20). Let us major on that!

The prosperity gospel blurs this abominably. It effectively masks it. Indeed, it addresses the wrong priority – the material instead of the spiritual. Consequently, it clashes badly with Christ's teaching, his law, delivered by the Lord to his people:

> Seek first the kingdom of God and his righteousness, and all these things [that is, the material benefits you need, not want] will be added to you. Therefore do not be anxious about tomorrow, for tomorrow will be anxious for itself. Sufficient for the day is its own trouble (Matt. 6:33-34).

No prosperity gospeller would have a punch line which talks of daily trouble for the godly man and woman. But Christ does. This is the climax of his teaching here. He declares that bliss is not to be found or sought by the believer in this life – leave that to the pagan – but in himself, the kingdom and eternity. In this life believers will have daily trouble, and they should not add to it by taking on board the anticipated trouble of tomorrow. 'Sufficient for the day is its own trouble'. As he later declared: 'In the world you will have tribulation. But take heart; I have overcome the world' (John 16:33). As Paul could assert with utter confidence, blazing abroad his assurance:

> If then you have been raised with Christ, seek the things that are above, where Christ is, seated at the right hand of

God. Set your minds on things that are above, not on things that are on earth. For you have died, and your life is hidden with Christ in God. When Christ who is your life appears, then you also will appear with him in glory (Col. 3:1-4).

Now that is the gospel!